Letters from

Correspondence of L. Hearn with Henry Watkin

Lafcadio Hearn

Editor: Milton Bronner

Alpha Editions

This edition published in 2022

ISBN : 9789356718401

Design and Setting By
Alpha Editions
www.alphaedis.com
Email - info@alphaedis.com

Introduction

It is felt that no apology is necessary for offering to the interested public, even though it be a limited one, the letters and extracts from letters which appear in this little volume. In a day when the letters of Aubrey Beardsley—who was a draughtsman rather than a writer—are gravely offered to possible readers by a great publishing house, it is surely allowable to present for the first time epistles of a really great author. No excuse was offered for printing such things as: "Thank you so much. It was very good of you to call." If this tells us anything concerning the unfortunate young master of white and black, I am unable to discern it. I feel quite sure that no one can make the same objection to the correspondence herewith given. It tells us many things concerning Hearn's life and moods and aspirations that otherwise would have been unknown to us. He wrote to Mr. Henry Watkin as to his dearest friend. In his letters, we get what we do not find elsewhere. We have here facts without which his future biographer would be at a loss.

If there be any repetitions in the sections which follow, the indulgence of the reader is craved. Such as they are, they were written at widely separated intervals in the hope that material might be finally gathered for a "Life and Letters of Hearn." This hope has so far been frustrated, but it is felt that much is here offered that will lead to a better understanding and appreciation of this famous writer. The endeavor of the editor has been so far as possible to let Hearn tell his own story, giving only enough comment to make clear what Hearn himself had to say.

In writing of their beloved R. L. S., enthusiasts tell us Stevenson is endeared to mankind not only because of his writings, but also because of his dauntless cheerfulness in the face of incurable disease. Hearn, in another field, was equally charming in his work and, in the face of another danger, equally dauntless. From the first he was confronted by the possible fate of the sightless. At best he had but a pearly vision of the world. The mere labor of writing was a physical task with him, demanding hours for the composition of a single letter. Yet he accomplished almost two score volumes, none of which is carelessly written. Seeing as through a ghostly vapor, in his books he revelled in color as few writers of our day have been able to do. How he managed to see, or rather to comprehend, all the things he so vividly described, was one of his secrets.

The best work of his life was commenced at the age of forty, when he arrived in Japan. He had many qualifications for his chosen field. During the long, lazy two years in Martinique he had literally soaked his mind, as it were, with Oriental philosophy. When he came to Japan he was weary of wandering, and the courtesy, gentleness and kindliness of the natives soon convinced him that they were the best people in the world among whom to live. A small man physically, he felt at home in a nation of small men. It pleased his shy, sensitive nature to think that he was often mistaken for a Japanese.

To his studies and his work he brought a prodigious curiosity, a perfect sympathy, and an admirable style. He had an eye that observed everything in this delightful Nippon, from the manner in which the women threaded their needles to the effect of Shinto and Buddhism upon the national character, religion, art, and literature. Japanese folk-lore, Japanese street songs and sayings, the home life of the people,—everything appealed to him, and the farther removed from modern days and from Christianity, the stronger the appeal.

Zangwill has acutely said, in speaking of Loti's famous story of Japan, "Instead of looking for the soul of a people, Pierre Loti was simply looking for a woman."

Hearn did not fail to tell us of many women, but his most particular search was for just that soul of a people which Loti ignored; and in the hunt for that soul, he became more and more impressed by that Buddhism which enabled him the better to comprehend the people. His whole religious life had been a wandering away from the Christianity to which he was born and a finding of a faith compounded of Buddhism modified by paganism, and a leaven of the scientific beliefs of agnostics such as Spencer and Huxley, whom he never wearied of reading and quoting. In all his writings this tendency is displayed. In one of the letters we see him an avowed agnostic, or perhaps "pantheist" would be the better word. In his little-known story of 1889, published in *Lippincott's*, with the Buddhist title of "Karma," there is a curious tribute to a fair, pure woman. It shows the hold the theory of heredity and evolution and the belief in reincarnation already had upon him:

"In her beauty is the resurrection of the fairest past;—in her youth, the perfection of the present;—in her girl dreams, the promise of the To-Be.... A million lives have been consumed that hers should be made admirable; countless minds have planned and toiled and agonized that thought might reach a higher and purer power in her delicate brain;—countless hearts have been burned out by suffering that hers might pulse for joy;— innumerable eyes have lost their light that hers might be filled with witchery;—innumerable lips have prayed that hers might be kissed." On his first day in the Orient he visited a temple and made an offering, recording the following conversation, which gives an admirable insight into his religious beliefs:[1]

"'Are you a Christian?'

"And I answered truthfully,'No.'

"'Are you a Buddhist?'

"'Not exactly.'

"'Why do you make offerings if you do not believe in Buddha?'

"'I revere the beauty of his teaching, and the faith of those who follow it.'"

From this by degrees he reached to a pure Buddhism, tempered, however, by a strange, romantic half belief, half love for the old pagan gods, feeling himself at heart a pagan, too:

"For these quaint Gods of Roads and Gods of Earth are really living still, though so worn and mossed and feebly worshipped. In this brief moment, at least, I am really in the Elder World,—perhaps just at that epoch of it when the primal faith is growing a little old-fashioned, crumbling slowly before the corrosive influence of a new philosophy; and I know myself a pagan still, loving these simple old gods, these gods of a people's childhood. And they need some love, these naïf, innocent, ugly gods. The beautiful divinities will live forever by that sweetness of womanhood idealized in the Buddhist art of them: eternal are Kwannon and Benten; they need no help of man; they will compel reverence when the great temples shall all have become voiceless and priestless as this shrine of Koshin is. But these kind, queer, artless, mouldering gods, who have given ease to so many troubled minds, who have gladdened so many simple hearts, who have heard so many innocent prayers,—how gladly would I prolong their beneficent lives in spite of the so-called 'laws of progress' and the irrefutable philosophy of evolution."

It is the combination of the various beliefs here shadowed that explains the unique note he brought into our literature. The man who was at once a follower of Spencer and of Buddha, with a large sympathy for the old folk-religion, brought forth an embodied thought entirely new to the world. Nothing like it had ever been produced before. Its like may never be produced again. He endeavored to reconcile the evolutional theory of inherited tendencies with the Buddhist belief in reincarnation,—one lengthening chain of lives,—and with the worship of the dead as seen in pure Shinto, for "is not every action indeed the work of the Dead who dwell within us?"

It was this queer combination that gave a strange charm, a moving magic, to various passages in his books. For the rest, his work and method of labor, may best be described in his own words when speaking of Japanese artists. He writes:

"The foreign artist will give you realistic reflections of what he sees; but he will give you nothing more. The Japanese artist gives you that which he feels,—the mood of a season, the precise sensation of an hour and place; his work is qualified by a power of suggestiveness rarely found in the art of the West. The Occidental painter renders minute detail; he satisfies the imagination he evokes. But his Oriental brother either suppresses or idealizes detail,—steeps his distances in mist, bands his landscapes with cloud, makes of his experience a memory in which only the strange and the beautiful survive, with their sensations. He surpasses imagination, excites it, leaves it hungry with the hunger of charm perceived in glimpses only. Nevertheless in such glimpses he is able to convey the feeling of a time, the character of a place, after a fashion that seems magical. He is a painter of recollections and sensations rather than of clear-cut realities; and in this lies the secret of his amazing power."

It has often been asked, "These books are beautiful as prose, but do they give us Japan?" Some have said he saw Japan with the eyes of a lover and was thus deceived. Captain F. Brinkley, an authority on Oriental matters and for years editor of the most important English paper in the Orient, has expressed, to the present writer, his skepticism concerning the entire verity of some of Hearn's pictures. On the other hand, here is what two Japanese writers say: Mr. Yone Noguchi, himself a poet of no mean abilities, writes of Hearn: "I like to vindicate Hearn from the criticism that his writing is about one third Japanese and two thirds Hearn. Fortunately his two thirds Hearn is also Japanese."

This is heartily seconded by Mr. Adachi Kinnosuke: "So truly did he write of us and of our land, that the West, which is always delighted to fall in love with counterfeits in preference to the genuine, did not believe him; made merry at his expense, told him that he was a dreamer, that his accounts were too rose-colored. We of the soil only marvelled. Of him we have said that he is more of Nippon than ourselves."

No fitter close to this introduction may be given than Noguchi's prose elegy sent to America from Tokio several days after Hearn's interment:

"Truly he was a delicate, easily broken Japanese vase, old as the world, beautiful as a cherry blossom. Alas! that wonderful vase was broken. He is no more with us. Surely we could better lose two or three battle-ships at Port Arthur than Lafcadio Hearn."

[1] This and several other extracts are from that delightful book, *Glimpses of Unfamiliar Japan*, Houghton, Mifflin & Co.

Letters from The Raven

Take up any book written by Lafcadio Hearn concerning Japan, and you will find the most delicate interpretation of the life of the people, their religion, their folk-songs, their customs, expressed in English that it is a delight to read. Upon further examination you will notice the calm, the serenity, the self-poise of the writer. It is as though, miraculously finding utterance, he were one of those stone Buddhas erected along the Japanese highways. He seems to have every attribute of a great writer save humor. There is hardly a smile in any of his books on Japan. One would say that the author was a man who never knew what gaiety was. One would judge that his life had lain in quiet places always, without any singular sorrow or suffering, without any struggle for existence. Judged by what Hearn told the world at large, the impression would be a correct one.

He was shy by nature. He did not take the world into his confidence. He was not one to harp on his own troubles and ask the world to sympathize with him. The world had dealt him some very hard blows,—blows which hurt sorely,—and so, while he gave the public his books, he kept himself to himself. He transferred the aroma of Japan to his writings. He did not sell the reader snap-shots of his own personality. To one man only perhaps in the whole world did the little Greek-Irishman reveal his inner thoughts, and he was one who thirty-eight years ago opened his heart and his home to the travel-stained, poverty-burdened lad of nineteen, who had run away from a monastery in Wales and who still had part of his monk's garb for clothing when he reached America.

Hearn never discussed his family affairs very extensively, but made it clear that his father was a surgeon in the crack Seventy-sixth Regiment of British Infantry, and his mother a Greek woman of Cherigo in the Ionian Islands. The social circle to which his father belonged frowned on the *mesalliance*, and when the wife and children arrived in England, after the father's death, the aristocratic relatives soon made the strangers feel that they were anything but welcome.

The young Lafcadio was chosen for the priesthood, and after receiving his education partly in France and partly in England, he was sent to a monastery in Wales. As he related afterwards, he was in bad odor there from the first. Even as a boy he had the skeptical notions about things religious that were to abide with him for long years after and change him to an ardent materialist until he fell under the influence of Buddhism. One day, after a dispute with the priests, and in disgust with the course in life that had been mapped out for him, the boy took what money he could get and made off to America. After sundry adventures, concerning which he was always silent, he arrived in Cincinnati in 1869, hungry, tired, unkempt,—a boy without a trade, without friends, without money. In some way he made the acquaintance of a Scotch printer, and this man in turn introduced him to Henry Watkin, an Englishman, largely self-educated, of broad culture and wide reading, of singular liberality of views, and a lover of his kind. Watkin at this time ran a printing shop.

Left alone with the lad, who had come across the seas to be as far away as possible from his father's people, the man of forty-five surveyed the boy of nineteen and said, "Well, my young man, how do you expect to earn a living?"

"I don't know."

"Have you any trade?"

"No, sir."

"Can you do anything at all?"

"Yes, sir; I might write," was the eager reply.

"Umph!" said Watkin; "better learn some bread-winning trade and put off writing until later."

After this Hearn was installed as errand boy and helper. He was not goodly to look upon. His body was unusually puny and under-sized. The softness of his tread had something feline and feminine in it. His head, covered with long black hair, was full and intellectual, save for two defects, a weak chin and an eye of the variety known as "pearl,"—large and white and bulbous, so that it repelled people upon a first acquaintance.

Hearn felt deeply the effect his shyness, his puny body, and his unsightly eye had upon people, and this feeling served to make him even more diffident and more melancholy than he was by nature. However, as with many melancholy-natured souls, he had an element of fun in him, which came out afterwards upon his longer acquaintance with the first man who had given him a helping hand.

Hearn swept the floor of the printing shop and tried to learn the printer's craft, but failed, He slept in a little room back of the shop and ate his meals in the place with Mr. Watkin. He availed himself of his benefactor's library, and read Poe and volumes on free thought, delighted to find a kindred spirit in the older man. Together they often crossed the Ohio River into Kentucky to hear lectures on spiritualism and laugh about them. Their companionship was not broken when Mr. Watkin secured for the boy a position with a Captain Barney, who edited and published a commercial, paper, for which Hearn solicited advertisements and to which he began also to contribute articles. One of these—a singular composition for such a paper—was a proposal to cross the Atlantic in a balloon anchored to a floating buoy. It was later in the year that he secured a position as a reporter on the *Enquirer*, through some "feature" articles he shyly deposited upon the editor's desk, making his escape before the great man had caught him in the act. It was not long before the latent talent in the youth began to make itself manifest. He was not a rapid writer. On the contrary, he was exceedingly slow, but his product was written in English that no reporter then working in Cincinnati approached. His fellow reporters soon became jealous of him. They were, moreover, repelled by his personal appearance and chilled by his steady refusal to see the fun of getting drunk. Finding lack of congeniality among the young men of his own age and occupation, among whom he was to work for seven more years, his friendship with Mr. Watkin became all the stronger, so that he came to look upon the latter as the one person in Cincinnati upon whom he could count for unselfish companionship and sincere advice. Hearn's Cincinnati experiences ended with his service on the *Enquirer*. Before that he had been proofreader to a publishing house and secretary to Cincinnati's public librarian. He was also for a time on the staff of the *Commercial.* It was while on the *Enquirer* that he accomplished several journalistic feats that are still referred to in gatherings of oldtime newspaper men of Cincinnati. One was a grisly description of the charred body of a murdered man, the screed being evidently inspired by recollections of Poe. The other was an article describing Cincinnati as seen from the top of a high church steeple, the joke of it being that Hearn, by reason of his defective vision, could see nothing even after he had made his perilous climb. It was in the last days of his stay in Cincinnati that he, with H. F. Farny, the painter, issued a short-lived weekly known as *Giglampz.* Farny, not yet famous as an Indian painter, contributed the drawings, and Hearn the bulk of the letter press for the journal, which modestly announced that it was going to eclipse *Punch* and all the other famous comic weeklies. Hearn, always sensitive, practically withdrew from the magazine when Farny took the very excusable liberty of changing the title of one of the essays of the former. Farny thought the title offensive to people of good taste, and said so. Hearn apparently acquiesced, but brooded over the "slight," and never again contributed to the weekly. Shortly afterwards it died. It is doubtful whether there are any copies in existence. Many Cincinnati collectors have made rounds of the second-hand book-shops in a vain search for stray numbers.

Early in their acquaintance Watkin and Hearn called each other by endearing names which were adhered to throughout the long years of their correspondence. Mr. Watkin, with his leonine head, was familiarly addressed as "Old Man" or "Dad;" while the boy, by virtue of his dark hair and coloring, the gloomy cast of his thoughts, and his deep love for Poe, was known as "The Raven," a name which caught his fancy. Indeed, a simple little drawing of the bird stood for many years in place of a signature to anything he chanced to write to Mr. Watkin. In spite of their varying lines of work, the two were often together. When "The Raven" was prowling the city for news, he was often accompanied by his "Dad." Not infrequently, when the younger man had no especial task, he would come to Mr. Watkin's office and read some books there. One of these, whose title and author Mr. Watkin has forgotten, fascinated at the same time that it repelled Hearn by its grim and ghastly stories of battle, murder, and sudden death. One night Mr. Watkin left him reading in the office. When he opened the place the next morning he found this note from Hearn:

"10 P.M. These stories are positively so horrible that even a materialist feels rather unpleasantly situated when left alone with the thoughts conjured up by this dreamer of fantastic dreams. The brain-chambers of fancy become thronged with goblins. I think I shall go home."

For signature there was appended a very black and a very thoughtful-looking raven.

It was also in these days that Hearn indulged in his little pleasantries with Mr. Watkin. Hardly a day passed without a visit to the printing office. When he did not find his friend, he usually left a card for him, on which was some little drawing, Hearn having quite a talent in this direction,-a talent that he never afterward developed. Of course some of the cards were just as nonsensical as the nonsense verses friends often write to each other. They are merely quoted to show Hearn's fund of animal spirits at the time.

A pencil sketch by Hearn left at Mr. Watkin's shop at the beginning of their friendship.

Mr. Watkin one day left a card for possible customers: "Gone to supper. H. W." Hearn passed by and wrote on the opposite side of the card: "Gone to get my sable plumage plucked." The inevitable raven followed as signature. It was Hearn's way of saying he had come to see Mr. Watkin and had then gone to a barber shop to have his hair cut. Once he omitted the raven and signed his note, "Kaw."

Facsimile of one of the cards Hearn left at Mr. Watkin's shop.

On another occasion when Mr. Watkin came to the office he found a note informing him that he was "a flabbergasted ichthyosaurus and an antediluvian alligator" for not being on hand.

The influence of Poe was strong upon him even in this nonsense. Hearn waited for his friend one night until a late hour. The shop was quite lonely, as it was the only open one in a big building on a more or less deserted street. The quiet became oppressive, and the little man left because "these chambers are cursed with the Curse of Silence. And the night, which is the Shadow of God, waneth."

Mr. Watkin had a dog. Hearn did not like the animal, and it seemed to reciprocate the feeling. One of Hearn's notes was largely devoted to the little beast. When he so chose Hearn could make a fairly good drawing. This particular note was adorned with rude pictures of an animal supposed to be a dog. The teeth were made the most prominent feature. The pictures were purposely made in a childish style, and used for the word "dog."

> "DEAR NASTY CROSS OLD MAN!
>
> "I tried to find you last night.
>
> "You were not in apparently.
>
> "I shook the door long and violently, and listened.
>
> "I did not hear the [dog] bark.
>
> "Perhaps you were not aware that the night you got so infernally mad I slipped a cooked beefsteak strongly seasoned with Strychnine under the door.
>
> "I was glad that the [dog] did not bark.

"I suspect the [dog] will not bark ANY MORE!

"I think the [dog] must have gone to that Bourne from which NO TRAVELLER RETURNETH.

"I hope the [dog] is DEAD."

The note is signed with the usual drawing of a raven. On still another occasion he wrote the following farrago:

"I came to see you—to thank you—to remonstrate with you—to demonstrate matters syllogistically and phlebotomically. GONE!!! Then I departed, wandering among the tombs of Memory, where the Ghouls of the Present gnaw the black bones of the Past. Then I returned and crept to the door and listened to see if I could hear the beating of your hideous heart."

These little notes are not presented here for any intrinsic merit; they are given simply to show how different was the real Hearn from the shy, silent, uncommunicative, grave, little reporter.

His notes were but precursors to the letters in which he was most truly to reveal himself. Unlike the epistles of great writers that so frequently find their way into print, Hearn's letters were not written with an eye to publication. They were written solely for the interest of their recipient. They were in the highest form of the true letter,—written talks with the favorite friend, couched usually in the best language the writer knew how to employ. They tell their own story,—the only story of Hearn's life,—a story often of hopeless search for bread-winning work; of bitter glooms and hysterical pleasures; of deep enjoyment of Louisiana autumns and West Indian and Japanese scenes; of savage hatred of Cincinnati and New Orleans, the two American cities in which he had worked as a newspaper man and in which he had been made to realize that he had many enemies and but few friends. Everything is told in these letters to Mr. Watkin, to whom he poured out his thoughts and feelings without reserve. Hearn's first step towards bettering himself followed when he became weary of the drudgery of work on the Cincinnati papers, and decided, after much discussion with Mr. Watkin, to resign his position and go South, the Crescent City being his objective point.

It was in October, 1877, that Hearn set out from Cincinnati on his way to New Orleans, going by rail to Memphis, whence he took the steamboat *Thompson Dean* down the Mississippi River to his destination. While in Memphis, impatiently waiting for his steamer to arrive, and afterwards in New Orleans, Hearn kept himself in touch with his friend in Cincinnati by means of a series of messages hastily scribbled on postal cards. Many of these reflected the animal spirits of the young man of twenty-seven, who had still preserved a goodly quantity of his boyishness, though he felt, as he said, as old as the moon. But not all of the little messages were gay. The tendency to despondency and morbidity, which had partially led Mr. Watkin to dub Hearn "The Raven," now showed itself. The first of these cards, which Mr. Watkin has preserved, was sent from Memphis on October 28, 1877. It bears two drawings of a raven. In one the eyes are very thoughtful. The raven is scratching its head with its claws, and below is the legend, "In a dilemma at Memphis." The other raven is merely labelled, "Remorseful." The next was sent on October 29. Hearn had begun to worry. He wrote:

"DEAR O. M. [Old Man]: Did not stop at Louisville. Could n't find out anything about train. Am stuck at Memphis for a week waiting for a boat. Getting d—d poor. New Orleans far off. Five hundred miles to Vicksburg. Board two dollars per day. Trouble and confusion. Flabbergasted. Mixed up. Knocked into a cocked hat."

The raven, used as the signature, wears a troubled countenance. On the same day, perhaps in the evening, Hearn sent still another card:

"DEAR O. M.: Have succeeded with enormous difficulty in securing accommodations at one dollar per diem, including a bed in a haunted room. Very blue. Here is the mosquito of these parts, natural size. [Hearn gives a vivid pencil drawing of one, two thirds of an inch long.] I spend my nights in making war upon him and my days in watching the murmuring current of the Mississippi and the most wonderful sunsets on the Arkansaw side that I ever saw. Don't think I should like to swim the Mississippi at this point. Perhaps the *Dean* may be here on Wednesday. I don't like Memphis at all, but cannot express my opinion in a postal card. They have a pretty fountain here—much better than that old brass candlestick in Cincinnati."

The next postal card was mailed on October 30, and contains one of the cleverest drawings of the series. Hearn says: "It has been raining all day, and I have had nothing to do but look at it. Half wish was back in Cincinnati."

Then follows a rude sketch of part of the Ohio River and its confluence with the Mississippi. A huddle of buildings represents Cincinnati. Another huddle represents Memphis. There stands the raven, his eyes bulging out of his head, looking at some object in the distance. The object is a huge snail which is leaving New Orleans and is labelled the *Thompson Dean.*

One of the finest of all the letters he wrote to Mr. Watkin was from Memphis. It is dated October 31, 1877. In this he made a prediction which afterwards came literally true. He seemed to foresee that, while in his loneliness he would write often to Mr. Watkin, once he became engrossed in his work and saw new sights and new faces, his letters would be written at greater intervals.

"DEAR OLD DAD: I am writing in a great big, dreary room of this great, dreary house. It overlooks the Mississippi. I hear the puffing and the panting of the cotton boats and the deep calls of the river traffic; but I neither hear nor see the *Thompson Dean*. She will not be here this week, I am afraid, as she only left New Orleans to-day.

Facsimile of a postal card sent from Memphis

"My room is carpetless and much larger than your office. Old blocked-up stairways come up here and there through the floor or down through the ceiling, and they suddenly disappear. There is a great red daub on one wall as though made by a bloody hand when somebody was staggering down the stairway. There are only a few panes of glass in the windows. I am the first tenant of the room for fifteen years. Spiders are busy spinning their dusty tapestries in every corner, and between the bannisters of the old stairways. The planks of the floor are sprung, and when I walk along the room at night it sounds as though Something or Somebody was following me in the dark. And then being in the third story makes it much more ghostly.

"I had hard work to get a washstand and towel put in this great, dreary room; for the landlord had not washed his face for more than a quarter of a century, and regarded washing as an expensive luxury. At last I succeeded with the assistance of the barkeeper, who has taken a liking to me.

"Perhaps you have seen by the paper that General N. B. Forrest died here night before last. To-day they are burying him. I see troops of men in grey uniforms parading the streets, and the business of the city is suspended in honor of the dead. And they are firing weary, dreary minute guns.

"I am terribly tired of this dirty, dusty, ugly town,—a city only forty years old, but looking old as the ragged, fissured bluffs on which it stands. It is full of great houses, which were once grand, but are now as waste and dreary within and without as the huge building in which I am lodging for the sum of twenty-five cents a night. I am obliged to leave my things in the barkeeper's care at night for fear of their being stolen; and he thinks me a little reckless because I sleep with my money under my pillow. You see the doors of my room—there are three of them—lock badly.... They are ringing those dead bells every moment,—it is a very unpleasant sound. I suppose you will not laugh if I tell you that I have been crying a good deal of nights,—just like I used to do when a college boy returned from vacation. It is a lonely feeling, this of finding oneself alone in a strange city, where you never meet a face that you know; and when all the faces you did know seem to have been dead faces, disappeared for an indefinite time. I have not travelled enough the last eight years, I suppose: it does not do to become attached insensibly to places and persons.... I suppose you have had some postal cards from me; and you are beginning to think I am writing quite often. I suppose I am, and you know the reason why; and perhaps you are thinking to yourself: 'He feels a little blue now, and is accordingly very affectionate, &c.; but by and by he will be quite forgetful, and perhaps will not write so often as at present.'

"Well, I suppose you are right. I live in and by extremes and am on an extreme now. I write extremely often, because I feel alone and extremely alone. By and by, if I get well, I shall write only by weeks; and with time perhaps only by months; and when at last comes the rush of business and busy newspaper work, only by years,—until the times and places of old friendship are forgotten, and old faces have become dim as dreams, and these little spider-threads of attachments will finally yield to the long strain of a thousand miles."

A postal card of November 3 says: "Will leave Memphis Tuesday next, PERHAPS. Am beginning to doubt the existence of the *Thompson Dean.*" November 13, 1877, finds Hearn overjoyed to be in New Orleans. The postal card bears in the left-hand corner a drawing of a door labelled "228." In a window at the side of the door sits the raven. On the other side is the legend:

Raven liveth at
228 Baronne St.
New Orleans
Care Mrs. Bustellos

Then comes another raven, with the doggerel:

Indite him an epistle.
Don't give him particular H—.

And finally the remarks:

Pretty Louisiana! Nice Louisiana!

Hearn began to send letters to one of the Cincinnati papers, but was soon in a terrible plight, as his postal card of December 9 demonstrates:

"I am in a very desperate fix here,—having no credit. If you can help me a little within the next few days, please try. I fear I must ask you to ask Davie to sell all my books except the French ones. The need of money has placed me in so humiliating a position that I cannot play the part of correspondent any longer. The *Commercial* has not sent me anything, and I cannot even get stamps. I landed in New Orleans with a fraction over twenty dollars, which I paid out in advance."

Facsimile of a postal card

Mr. Watkin was unable to make the reply he desired, and was even prevented by other matters from answering in any way until weeks later. It was this silence which caused Hearn to mail a postal card, on January 13, 1878, which contained one of his cleverest drawings. In the background is shown the sky with a crescent moon. In the foreground, upright from a grass-grown, grave, stands a tombstone, bearing the inscription:

H. W.
DIED
NOV. 29
1877

Perched on top of the stone is a particularly ragged and particularly black raven. It was the last gleam of fun that was to come from him for some time. He was to experience some of the bitterest moments of his life, moments which explained his hatred of New Orleans, as the slanders of the newspapermen of Cincinnati embittered him against that city.

The following seems to be the first, or one of the first, letters written by him after his arrival in New Orleans. As usual, it is undated:

"DEAR OLD FRIEND: I cannot say how glad I was to hear from you. I did not—unfortunately—get your letter at Memphis; it would have cheered me up. I am slowly, very slowly, getting better.

Drawing on a postal card sent to Watkin to remind him he had not written

"The wealth of a world is here,—unworked gold in the ore, one might say; the paradise of the South is here, deserted and half in ruins. I never beheld anything so beautiful and so sad. When I saw it first—sunrise over Louisiana—the tears sprang to my eyes. It was like young death,—a dead bride crowned with orange flowers,—a dead face that asked for a kiss. I cannot say how fair and rich and beautiful this dead South is. It has fascinated me. I have resolved to live in it; I could not leave it for that chill and damp Northern life again. Yes; I think you could make it pay to come here. One can do much here with very little capital. The great thing is, of course, the sugar-cane business. Everybody who goes into it almost does well. Some make half a million a year at it. The capital required to build a sugar mill, &c., is of course enormous; but men often begin with a few acres and become well-to-do in a few years. Louisiana thirsts for emigrants as a dry land for water. I was thinking of writing to tell you that I think you could do something in the way of the fruit business to make it worth your while to comedown,—oranges, bananas, and tropical plants sell here at fabulously low prices. Bananas are of course perishable freight when ripe; but oranges are not, and I hear they sell at fifty cents a hundred, and even less than that a short distance from the city. So there are many other things here one could speculate in. I think with one partner North and one South, a firm could make money in the fruit business here. But there, you know I don't know anything about business. What's the good of asking ME about business?

"If you come here, you can live for almost nothing. Food is ridiculously cheap,—that is, cheap food. Then there are first-class restaurants here, where the charge is three dollars for dinner. But board and lodging is very cheap....

Facsimile of envelope addressed to Mr. Watkin by Hearn

"I have written twice to the *Commercial,* but have only seen one of my letters,—the Forrest letter. I have a copy. I fear the other letters will not be published. Too enthusiastic, you know. But I could not write coolly about beautiful Louisiana....

"Oh, you must come to New Orleans sometime,—no nasty chill, no coughs and cold. The healthiest climate in the world. Eternal summer.

"It is damp at nights however, and fires are lit of evenings to dry the rooms. You know the land is marshy. Even the dead are unburied,—they are only vaulted up. The cemeteries are vaults, not graveyards. Only the Jews bury their dead; and their dead are buried in water. It is water three—yes, two— feet underground.

"I like the people, especially the French; but of course I might yet have reason to change my opinion....

"Would you be surprised to hear that I have been visiting my UNCLE? Would you be astonished to learn that I was on the verge of poverty? No. Then, forsooth, I will be discreet. One can live here for twenty cents a day—what's the odds? ...

"Yours truly,

On the reverse side of an application for a money order, Hearn wrote to Watkin in 1878, some considerable time after his arrival in New Orleans:

"I see the Cincinnati *Commercial* once in a while, and do not find any difference in it. My departure affecteth its columns not at all. In sooth a man on a daily newspaper is as a grain of mustard seed. Hope I may do better in New Orleans. It is time for a fellow to get out of Cincinnati when they begin to call it the Paris of America. But there are some worse places than Cincinnati. There is Memphis, for example."

At one period, early during his stay in New Orleans, when Hearn began to look back upon what he had accomplished, or rather had failed to accomplish, in his life, he sank into the depths of despair. As was his wont, he wrote from his heart to his sole friend, depending upon him not only for cheer, but for advice. Mr. Watkin refused to take this long letter seriously, teased him about it rather, and advised him not to go to England, but to remain here in this country and persist in one line of work. The Hearn letter, which follows, belongs to the month of February, 1878:

"DEAR OLD MAN: I shall be twenty-eight years old in a few days,—a very few days more; and I am frightened to think how few they are. I am afraid to look at the almanac to find out what day The Day falls upon,—it might fall upon a Friday,—and I can't shake off a superstition about it,—a superstition always outlives a religion. Looking back at the file of these twenty-eight years, which grow more shadowy in receding, I can remember and distinguish the features of at least twenty. There is an alarming similarity of misery in all their faces; and however misty the face, the outlines of misery are remarkably perceptible. Each, too, seems to be a record of similar events,—thwarting of will and desire in every natural way, ill success in every aim, denial of almost every special wish, compulsion to ad upon the principle that everything agreeable was wrong and everything disagreeable right, unpleasant recognition of selfweakness and inability to win success by individual force,—not to mention enormous addenda in the line of novel and wholly unexpected disappointments. Somehow or other, whenever I succeeded in an undertaking, the fruit acquired seemed tasteless and vapid; but usually, when one step more would have been victory, some extraordinary and unanticipated obstacle rose up in impassability. I must acknowledge, however, that, as a general rule, the unexpected obstacle was usually erected by myself;—some loss of temper, impatience, extra-sensitiveness, betrayed and indulged instead of concealed, might be credited with a large majority of failures.

"Without a renovation of individuality, however, I really can see no prospect, beyond the twenty-eighth year, of better years—the years seem to

- 18 -

grow worse in regular succession. As to the renovation,—it is hardly possible: don't you think so? Sometimes I think small people without great wills and great energies have no business trying to do much in this wonderful country; the successful men all appear to have gigantic shoulders and preponderant deportments. When I look into the private histories of the young men who achieved success in the special line I have been vainly endeavoring to follow to some termination, I find they generally hanged themselves or starved to death, while their publishers made enormous fortunes and world-wide reputations after their unfortunate and idealistic customers were dead. There were a few exceptions, but these exceptions were cases of extraordinary personal vigor and vital force. So while my whole nature urges me to continue as I have begun, I see nothing in prospect: except starvation, sickness, artificial wants, which I shall never be wealthy enough to even partially gratify, and perhaps utter despair at the end. Then again, while I have not yet lost all confidence in myself, I feel strongly doubtful whether I shall ever have means or leisure to develop the latent (possible) ability within me to do something decently meritorious. Perhaps, had I not been constrained to ambition by necessity, I should never have had any such yearnings about the unattainable and iridescent bubbles of literary success. But that has nothing to do with the question. Such is the proposition now: how can I get out of hell when I have got halfway down to the bottom of it? Can I carry on any kind of business? I can fancy that I see you throw back your head and wag your beard with a hearty laugh at the mere idea, the preposterous idea!

"Can I keep any single situation for any great length of time? You know I can't,—couldn't stand it; hate the mere idea of it,—something horribly disagreeable would be sure to happen. Then again, I can't even stay in one place for any healthy period of time. I can't stay anywhere without getting in trouble. And my heart always feels like a bird, fluttering impatiently for the migrating season. I think I could be quite happy if I were a swallow and could have a summer nest in the ear of an Egyptian colossus or a broken capital of the Parthenon.

"I know just exactly what I should like to do,—to wander forever here and there until I got very old and apish and grey, and died,—just to wander where I pleased and keep myself to myself, and never bother anybody. But that I can't do. Then what in the name of the Nine Incarnations of Vishnu, can I do? Please try to tell me.

"Shall I, in spite of myopia, seek for a passage on some tropical vessel, and sail hither and thither on the main, like the ghost of Gawain on a wandering wind, till I have learned all the ropes and spars by heart, and know by sight the various rigging of all the navies of the world?

"Shall I try to go back to England at once, instead of waiting to be a millionaire? (This is a seaport, remember: that is why I dread to leave it for further inland towns. I feel as if I could almost catch a distant glimpse of the mighty dome of St. Paul's from the levee of New Orleans.)

"Shall I begin to eat opium, and enjoy in fancy all that reality refuses, and may forever refuse me?

"Shall I go to Texas and start a cheap bean-house—(hideous occupation!) with my pact, who wants me to go there?

"Shall I cease to worry over fate and facts, and go right to hell on a 2.40, till I get tired even of hell and blow my highly sensitive and exquisitely delicate brains out?

"Shall I try to get acquainted with Yellow Jack and the Charity Hospital,—or try to get to St. Louis on the next boat? Honestly, I'd like to know. I'm so tired,—so awfully, fearfully, disgustingly tired of wasting my life without being able to help it. Don't tell me I could have helped it,—I know better. No man could have helped doing anything already done. I hate the gilded slavery of newspaper work,—the starvation of Bohemianism,—the bore of waiting for a chance to become an insurance agent or a magazine writer,—and oh, venerable friend, I hate a thousand times worst of all to work for somebody else. I hoped to become independent when I came down here,—to work for myself; and I have made a most damnable failure of it. In addition to the rest, my horrid eye is bad yet. I had lost nearly half the field of vision from congestion of the retina when I wrote you the rather frantic epistles which you would not answer. Now I see only in patches, but am getting along better and hope to be quite well in time,—certainly much better. You see I can write a pretty long letter to while away Sunday idleness."

Hearn had reached New Orleans at the time the yellow fever was raging there, and in April, 1878, he wrote reassuring his old friend that his health was not endangered:

"DEAR OLD MAN: Yellow Jack has not caught me; and since I was laid up with the dengue or break-bone fever, I believe I am acclimated.... They sprinkle the streets here with watering-carts filled with carbolic acid, pour lime in the gutters, and make all the preparations against fever possible, except the only sensible one of cleaning the stinking gutters and stopping up the pest-holes. Politicians make devilish bad health officers. When I tell you that all of our gutters are haunted by eels whose bite is certain death, you can imagine how vile they are.... Nobody works here in summer. The population would starve to death anywhere else. Neither does anybody think of working in the sun if they can help it. That is why we have no sunstroke. The horses usually wear hats."

After a seven months' hunt for work Hearn saw some of the hardest times of his life in New Orleans. The situation, as he described in his letter to Mr. Watkin, could not have been worse than when, as a waif, he wandered the streets of London. It was postmarked June 14, 1878.

"DEAR OLD MAN: Wish you would tell me something wise and serviceable. I'm completely and hopelessly busted up and flattened out, but I don't write this because I have any desire to ask you for pecuniary assistance,—have asked for that elsewhere. Have been here seven months and never made one cent in the city. No possible prospect of doing anything in this town now or within twenty-five years. Books and clothes all gone, shirt sticking through seat of my pants,—literary work rejected East,—get a five-cent meal once in two days,—don't know one night where I'm going to sleep next,—and am d—d sick with climate into the bargain. Yellow fever supposed to be in the city. Newspapers expected to bust up. Twenty dollars per month is a good living here; but it's simply impossible to make even ten. Have been cheated and swindled considerably; and have cheated and swindled others in retaliation. We are about even. D—n New Orleans!— wish I'd never seen it. I am thinking of going to Texas. How do you like the idea?—to Dallas or Waco. Eyes about played out, I guess. Have a sort of idea that I can be wonderfully economical if I get any more good luck. Can save fifteen out of twenty dollars a month—under new conditions (?). Have no regular place of residence now. Can't you drop a line to P. O. next week, letting shining drops of wisdom drip from the end of your pen?"

It was right after this in the same month, when his fortunes were at the lowest ebb, that things took a turn for the better, as is indicated by the following, in which in jest he proposes to engage in a "get-rich-quick" scheme:

"DEAR OLD MAN: Somehow or other, when a man gets right down in the dirt, he jumps up again. The day after I wrote you, I got a position (without asking for it) as assistant editor on the *Item*, at a salary considerably smaller than that I received on the *Commercial* (of Cincinnati), but large enough to enable me to save half of it. Therefore I hasten to return Will's generous favor with the most sincere thanks and kindest wishes. You would scarcely know me now, for my face is thinner than a knife and my skin very dark. The Southern sun has turned me into a mulatto. I have ceased to wear spectacles, and my hair is wild and ghastly. I am seriously thinking of going into a fraud, which will pay like hell,—an advertising fraud: buying land by the pound and selling it in boxes at one dollar per box. I have a party here now who wants to furnish bulk of capital and go shares. He is an old hand at the dodge. It would be carried along under false names, of course; and there is really no money in honest work.... I think I shall see you in the fall or spring; and when I come again to Cincinnati, it will be, my dear old man, as you would wish, with money in my pocket. It did me much good to hear from you; for I fancied my postal card asking for help might have offended you; and I feared you had resolved that I was a fraud. Well, I am something of a fraud, but not to everybody I don't like the people here at all, and would not live here continually. But it is convenient now, for I could not live cheaper elsewhere."

Again undated, but belonging to his early New Orleans period, is the letter in which, after discussing some business venture he had in mind, he says:

"There is a strong feeling down here that the South will soon be the safest place to live in. The labor troubles North promise to be something terrible. I assure you that few well-posted newspaper men here would care to exchange localities until after these labor troubles have assumed some definite shape. There is no labor element here that is dangerous.

"There are some businesses which would pay here: a cheap restaurant, a cheap swimming bath, or a cheap laundry. Money just now could be coined at any of these things. Everything else here is dead. I met a highly educated Jew here not long ago, who had lived and made money in New Zealand, Martinique, British Columbia, Panama, Sandwich Islands, Buenos Ayres, and San Francisco. 'I have been,' he said, 'almost every place where money can be made, and I know almost every dodge known to Hebrews in the money-making way. But I do not see a single chance to make anything in this town.' He left for the North. He was from London.

"I should like to see you down here, if it were not for malaria. You would not escape the regular marsh fever; but that is not dangerous when the symptoms are recognized and promptly treated. When I had it I did not know what it was. I took instinctively a large dose of castor oil. Sometime after I met the druggist, a good old German, who sold it me. 'I never expected to see you again,' he said; 'you had a very bad case of fever when I saw you.'

"But everybody gets that here. You live so abstemiously and thirst so little after the flesh-pots that I think you would not have much to fear. I go swimming a good deal; but I find the water horribly warm. The lake seems to be situated directly over the great furnace of Hell....

"I'll be doubly d——d if I have the vaguest idea what I shall do. I have a delightfully lazy life here; and I assure you I never intend to work fourteen hours a day again. But whether to leave here I don't know. I'm only making about ten dollars a week, but that is better than making twenty-five dollars and being a slave to a newspaper. I write what I please, go when I please, and quit work when I please. I have really only three hours a day office duty,—mostly consumed in waiting for proofs. If I stay here, I can make more soon. But I don't really care a damn whether I make much money or not. If I have to make money by working hard for it, I shall certainly remain poor. I have done the last hard work I shall ever do.

"On the success of some literary work, however, I have a vague idea of receiving enough ready money to invest in some promising little specs, here,—of the nature I have already hinted at. If they pay, they will pay admirably. If I lose the money, I shan't die of starvation....

"I shall certainly not leave here before seeing Cuba. It would be a mortal sin to be so near the Antilles and yet never have sailed that sapphire sea yclept the Spanish Main.

"I never felt so funny in my whole life. I have no ambition, no loves, no anxieties,—sometimes a vague unrest without a motive, sometimes a feeling as if my heart was winged and trying to soar away, sometimes a vague longing for pleasurable wanderings, sometimes a halfcrazy passion for a great night with wine and women and music. But these are much like flitting dreams, and amount to little. They are ephemeral. The wandering passion is strongest of all; and I feel no inclination to avail myself of the only anchor which keeps the ship of a man's life in port.

"Then again,—I have curiously regained memories of long ago, which I thought utterly forgotten. Leisure lends memory a sharp definition. Life here is so lazy,—nights are so liquid with tropic moonlight,—days are so splendid with green and gold,—summer is so languid with perfume and warmth,—that I hardly know whether I am dreaming or awake. It is all a dream here, I suppose, and will seem a dream even after the sharp awakening of another voyage, the immortal gods only know where. Ah! Gods! beautiful Gods of antiquity! One can only feel you, and know you, and believe in you, after living in this sweet, golden air. What is the good of dreaming about earthly women, when one is in love with marble, and ivory, and the bronzes of two thousand years ago? Let me be the last of the idol-worshippers, O golden Venus, and sacrifice to thee the twin doves thou lovest,—the birds of Paphos,—the Cythendae!"

Hearn had had his troubles with New Orleans and Cincinnati newspaper men, some of whom pirated his translations, while others printed slanderous stories concerning his manner of living,—slanders which Mr. Watkin combated in a personal letter to the editor of the *Commercial* some years after, when his attackers again became busy. On July 10, 1878, Hearn wrote:

"MY DEAR OLD MAN: Was delighted to hear from you. I am very glad the thing is as much of a mystery to you as it is to me. I can only surmise that it must have been a piece of spite work on the part of a certain gentleman connected with the N. O. *Times,* who printed some of my work before, and got a raking for it. My position here is a peculiar one, and not as stable as I should like, so that if it were made to appear that I had re-utilized stuff from the *Item,* I would certainly get into trouble. I have been very ill for a week, break-bone fever. I do not expect to return North 'broke.' 'Cahlves is too scace in dis country to be killed for a prodigal son.' I wish you were near that I might whisper projects of colossal magnitude in your ear. I am working like hell to make a good raise for Europe. Will write more soon. Editor away to-day and the whole paper on my hands.

"*Monday.* Delayed posting letter. I find this climate terribly enervating. No one could have led a more monastic life than I have done here; yet I find I cannot even think energetically. The mind seems to lose all power of activity. I have been collecting materials for magazine articles, and I can't write them out. I have only been able to do mechanical work,—translating, &c., and one Romanesque essay, which was successively rejected by three magazines. Wish I was on a polar expedition.

"I have been an awfully good boy down here, and have no news to tell you of amours or curious experiences."

Hearn once more tells of his trouble with a Cincinnati paper, alleging the owners failed to pay him for his New Orleans correspondence, and how finally he was "happily discharged."

Then he resumes: "By the way, I wrote a poem for the decoration of the soldiers' graves at Chalmette National Cemetery, on the 30th inst. I think it was. The poem was read by Col. Wright of this city at the decoration and published in the *Democrat.* It was the first bit of rhyme I wrote, and so you must excuse it. But it is not as good as—

"*The love of Hearn and Watkin,*
What is its kin?—
It is two toads encysted
Within one stone,
Two vipers twisted
Into one.

"Here is the poem:

"*Fairflowers pass away:*
In perfumed ruin falls the lily's urn;
In pallid pink decay
Moulders the rose;—all in their time return

To the primeval clay.

"Yet still their tiny ghosts
Hover about our homes on viewless wings;
In incense-breathing hosts
They love to haunt those stores of trifling things
Of which affection boasts,—

"Some curl of glossy hair,—
Some loving letter penned by pretty fingers,—
Some volume old and rare,
On whose time-yellow fly-leaf fondly lingers
The name of a woman fair.

"So in that hour
When brave lives fail and brave hearts cease to beat,—
Each deed of power
Lives on to haunt our memories,—faintly sweet
Like the ghost of a flower.

"Each flower we strew
In tribute to the brave to-day shall prove
A token true
Of some sweet memory of the dead we love,—
The Men in Blue.

"Perchance the story
Of Chalmette's heroes may be lost to fame,
As years wax hoary;
But Valor's Angel keeps each gallant name
On his Roll of Glory."

August 14, 1878, Hearn wrote a letter to the man who had always cheered him and who now in turn needed cheering. Business in all lines in Cincinnati was bad, and Mr. Watkin was quite despondent. He had written Hearn something of this, and also had hinted that he might move to Kansas or somewhere farther West. In return he received the following letter, expressive of all that was most fun-loving in its writer:

"MY DEAR OLD MAN: I think you had better come here next Oktober and rejoin your naughty raven. It would not do you any harm to reconnoitre. Think of the times we could have,—delightful rooms with five large windows opening on piazzas shaded by banana trees; dining at Chinese restaurants and being served by Manila waitresses, with oblique eyes and skin like gold; visiting sugar-cane plantations; scudding over to Cuba; dying with the mere delight of laziness; laughing at cold and smiling at the news of snowstorms a thousand miles away; eating the cheapest food in the world,—and sinning the sweetest kind of sins. Now you know, good old Dad, nice old Dad,—you know that you are lazy and ought to be still lazier. Come here and be lazy. Let me be the siren voice enticing a Ulysses who does not stuff wax in his ears. Don't go to horrid, dreadful Kansas. Go to some outrageous ruinous land, where the moons are ten times larger than they are there. Or tell me to pull up stakes, and I shall take unto myself the wings of a bird and fly to any place but beastly Cincinnati.

"Money can be made here out of the poor. People are so poor here that nothing pays except that which appeals to poverty. But I think you could make things hop around lively. Now one can make thirty milk biscuits for five cents and eight cups of coffee for five cents. Just think of it! ...

"Cincinnati is bad; but it's going to be a d—d sight worse. You know that as well as I do. Leave the vile hole and the long catalogue of Horrid Acquaintances behind you, and come down here to your own little man,— good little man. Get you nice room, nice board, nice business. Perhaps we might strike ile in a glorious spec. Why don't you spec.? You'd better spec, pretty soon, or the times will get so bad that you will have to get up and dust. This is a seaport. There are tall ships here. They sail to Europe,—to London, Marseilles, Constantinople, Smyrna. They sail to the West Indies and those seaports where we are going to open a cigar store or something of that kind.

Oh, I have seven tall ships at sea,
And seven more at hand;
And five and twenty jolly, jolly seamen
Shall be at your command.

May the Immortal Gods preserve you in immortal youth."

There now follow some letters whose dates it has been impossible to fix. The cancellation marks on the envelopes give the months, but not the years. However, there is internal evidence to show that they belong to the period between the last group and the group of 1882, so that they were written in the years 1879, 1880, and 1881, in all probability. The first is one of the most interesting letters in the whole set. The future great writer is displayed as the owner of a five-cent eating-house. The letter is replete with ridiculous little sketches of a bird, which he claimed was a raven. In fact:, in the following, wherever "raven" is used, the reader must understand that there is a drawing of one in the letter. It was written in February:

"MY DEAR O. M.: Your style of correspondence—four letters a year—leads me to suppose that the fate of the Raven is of little consequence. It was therefore with surprise that I heard of a letter concerning It being received at the *Item* office. The letter warranted the assumption that you had at least some curiosity, if nothing better, in regard to It. That curiosity should be gratified. The Raven keepeth a restaurant in the city of New Orleans. It is secretly in business for itself. It is also in the newspaper business. The reason It has gone into business for itself is that It is tired of working for other people. The reason that It is still in the newspaper line is that the business is not yet paying, and needs some financial support. The business is the cheapest in N. O. All dishes are five cents. Knocks the market price out of things. The business has already cost about one hundred dollars to set up. May pay well; may not. The Raven has a partner,—a large and ferocious man, who kills people that disagree with their coffee. The Raven expects to settle in Cuba before long. Is going there to reconnoitre in a few months,—if Fortune smileth. It has mastered the elements of Spanish language, and has a Spanish tutor who comes every day to teach It. It has been studying Spanish assiduously for six mos.; and trusts to be able to establish a *meson de los estrangeros*, or stranger's restaurant, in Havana,—unless It is busted up pretty soon. It might be busted up. As yet It has remained poor. Economy is the cause thereof. It has seen little of wine and women in this city. Its notions are mean and stingy. It is constantly suspicious that Its partner may go back on It. It is of a suspicious character. It has debts on its mind, but prefers to look after its own interests at present,—until It can buy some clothes. It also proposes to establish another five-cent eating-house here in the French quarter, sooner or later, if this one pays. If the O. M. ever leaves Cincinnati, he may see the Raven. Otherwise he will not. If he comes to this part of the world, he can obtain board cheap at the five-cent restaurant. The Raven would not object: to see him again,—on the contrary, he is filled with CURIOSITY to see him. The Raven may succeed right off. He may not. But he is going to succeed sooner or later, even if he has to start an eating-house in Hell. He sends you his respects,—reserving his affection for a later time."

Hearn enclosed with the latter a yellow handbill advertising his restaurant. It was as follows:

"The 5 cent Restaurant
160 Dryades Street

This is the cheapest eating-house in the South. It is neat, orderly, and respectable as any other in New Orleans. You can get a good meal for a couple of nickels. All dishes 5 cents. A large cup of pure Coffee, with Rolls, only 5 cents.

Everything half the price of the markets."

In a letter postmarked June 27, he again refers to his knowledge of Spanish, and, what is more interesting, makes his first reference to Japan, the country where he was to achieve his best work: "Your little Raven talks Spanish. Has a fair acquaintance with the language. Just now rusty for want of practice. Soon pick it up again.... "Have also wild theories regarding Japan.

Splendid field in Japan Climate just like

England,—perhaps a little milder. Plenty of Europeans. English, American and French papers....

"Would not be surprised if you could make N. Orleans trip pay—now that I have seen your circulars. Only—remember C. O. D. Everybody here is a thief. Must be careful even in changing a quarter not to get counterfeits or false change. Horrid den of villains, robbers, mutual admiration,—political quacks, medical quacks, literary quacks,—adventurers, Spanish, Italian, Greek, English, Corsican, French, Venezuelan,—Parisian roués, Sicilian murderers, Irish ruffians.... Couldn't be half so bad in Japan."

The censure of New Orleans people must not be taken too seriously. He afterwards had some very dear friends there, who changed his opinions to a great extent. On November 24 came a letter liberally sprinkled with drawings of the raven and replete with his fun:

"DEAR OLD MAN: The Raven has not found letter-writing a pleasant occupation lately. It has had some trouble; It has also been studying very hard; It has had Its literary work doubled, and It has had little leisure time, as Its grotesque and fantastic Eye is not yet in a healthy condition. It cannot write at night, not in these beautiful Southern Nights, which flame with stars,—the 'holy Night,' as the old Greek poet called it, which is 'all Eye, all Ear, all perfume to the student.'

"The Raven would like to see you, as It could tell you a great many queer things about Southern matters, which no paper has published or dare publish, and about the city and about the people. But It hardly hopes to see you; for after this summer It will not be here. It has latterly heard much of advantages held out to It in Mexico City, where the great exposition is soon to be held; and Its Spanish studies have been successful. It wants to find a temporary resting-place among Spanish people, and cannot stay here. It would be pleased to forget Its own language for a while, whether in Cuba or elsewhere.... The Raven cannot go North, as It cannot afford to. It will require all It can save to carry It through troubles which await It somewhere else,—for thou knowest full well that Woe is the normal condition of the Raven's existence. The Raven passeth Its time thusly: In the morning It a-riseth with the Sun and drinketh a cup of coffee and devoureth a piece of bread. Then It proceeded to the office and concocteth devilment for the *Item*, Then It returned to Its room, whose windows are shadowed by creeping plants and clouds of mosquitoes, and received Its Spanish tutor. Then It goeth to a Chinese restaurant, where It eateth an amazing dinner,—Its bump of ALIMENTATIVENESS being enormously developed. Then It spendeth two hours among the second-hand bookstores. It then goeth to bed,—to arise in the dead vast and middle of the night and smoke Its pipe. For a year It hath not smoked a cigar; and Its morals are exemplary. It sendeth you Its affectionate good-will and proceedeth forthwith to smoke Its pipe."

Again, without any clue as to its date and without any aid from the memory of Mr. Watkin, is a small photograph of the writer, with this characteristic note:

"DEAR OLD DAD: Would like to hear from you, to see you, to chat with you. Write me a line or two. As soon as I can find time, will write a nice, long, chatty letter,—all about everything you would like to hear. Am doing well. New Orleans is not, however, what I hoped it was. Are you well and happy? I have thoughts of cemeteries and graves, and a dear old Ghost with a white beard,—a Voice of the Past.

"I press your hand.

"LAFCADIO HEARN"

Facsimile of part of a letter from hearn to Mr. Watkin

Facsimile of a characteristic note from Hearn to mr. Watkin written on the back of a photograph

In a letter dated July 7, 1882, Hearn tells of his first adventures in the book-writing line and of the horrified criticisms of some of the Eastern book-reviewers. All told, however, he becomes the more purposeful Hearn, the man Mr. Watkin had always predicted he would be if he continued at his literary work in his own way. It is interesting for another reason, too, in that it shows how already, in these New Orleans days, Hearn was preparing himself by his studies for his future life in Japan.

"MY DEAR OLD DAD: Your letter lies before me here like a white tablet of stone bearing a dead name; and in my mind there is just such a silence as one feels standing before a tomb,—so that I can press your hand only and say nothing.

A fanciful pencil sketch by Hearn

"I must go North in a few months, by way of Cincinnati, and spend a week or so in the city. My intention is to see Worthington about a new publication. He is now in Europe. Here I make thirty dollars a week for about five hours' work a day, and the position appears tolerably solid; but the climate is enervating, the man who refuses to connect himself with church or clique lives alone like a hermit in the Thebaids, and one sickens of such a life at times. Sometimes I fancy that the older I grow, the more distasteful companionship becomes; but this may be owing to the situation here. Nevertheless I am feeling very old, old almost as the Tartar of Longfellow's poem,—'three hundred and sixty years.'

"Imagine the heavy, rancid air of a Southern swamp in midsummer, when the very clouds seem like those which belonged to the atmosphere of pregeologic periods, uncreated lead and iron,—never a breath of pure air,—dust that is powdered dung,—quaking ground that shakes with the passage of a wagon,—heat as of a perpetual vapor bath,—and at night, subtle damps that fill the bones with rheumatism and poison the blood. Then, when one thinks of green hills and brisk winds, comes a strange despondency. It is something like the outlying region through which Milton's Lucifer passed, half crawling, half flying, on his way to the Garden of Eden. Your little reprints provoked very pleasant old memories. I paid the Somebody one hundred and fifty dollars for the publication.[1] Have not yet heard from him. The understanding is that I get my money back and something besides. However, I shall be satisfied with the something. I have had many nice notices, letters from authors of some note, and a few criticisms of the true Pharisaic species. I enclose one for your amusement. I have also built up a fine library, about three hundred picked volumes, and have a little money saved. Have also some ambition to try the book business,—not here, but in San Francisco or somewhere else. However, I have no definite plans,—only a purpose to do something for myself and thus obtain leisure for a systematic literary purpose. Were you situated like me,—that is, having no large business or large interests,—I think I should try to coax you to seek the El Dorado of the future, where fortunes will certainly be made by practical men,—Mexico,—where no one ever lights a fire, and where one has only to go in the sun when he is too cold, into the shade when he is too warm. But for the present I will only ask you to come down here when the weather gets healthy and your business will allow it. You will stay with me, of course, and no expense. The trip would be agreeable in the season when the air is sweet with orange blossoms.

[1] Translation of Gautier's short stories.

"The population here is exceedingly queer,—something it is hard to describe, and something which it is possible to learn only after a painful experience of years. At present I may say that all my acquaintances here are limited to about half a dozen, with one or two friends whom I invite to see me occasionally. Yet almost daily I receive letters from people I do not know, asking favors which I never grant. New Orleans is the best school for the study of human selfishness I have ever been in. Buddhism teaches that the second birth is to this life 'as the echo to the voice in the cavern, as the great footprints to the steps of the elephant.' According to the teaching of the Oriental Christ, this whole population will be born again as wild beasts,—which is consoling. ... You say you cannot write. I differ with you; but it would certainly be impossible for either of us to write many things we would like to say. Still, you can easily drop a line from time to time, even a postal card, just to let me know you are well. If I do not get up to see you by September, I hope to see you down. I dreamed one night that I heard the ticking of the queer clock,—like the longstrides of a man booted and spurred. You know the clock I mean,—the long, weird-faced clock. My eyes are not well, of course,—never will be; but they are better. More about myself I cannot tell you in a letter,—except that I suppose I have changed a little. Less despondent, but less hopeful; wiser a little and more silent; less nervous, but less merry; more systematic and perhaps a good deal more selfish. Not strictly economical, but coming to it steadily; and in leisure hours studying the theories of the East, the poetry of antique India, the teachings of the wise concerning absorption and emanation, the illusions of existence, and happiness as the equivalent of annihilation. Think they were wiser than the wisest of Occidental ecclesiastics.

"And still there is in life much sweetness and much pleasure in the accomplishment of a fixed purpose. Existence may be a delusion and desire a snare, but I expect to exist long enough to satisfy my desire to see thee again before entering Nirvana. So, reaching to thee the grasp of friendship across the distance of a thousand miles, I remain in the hope of being always remembered sincerely as your friend."

On September 10, 1882, in reply to a letter from Mr. Watkin, in which the latter said he thought of going to Tampa for a rest and possibly also to look around and see what the business prospers were, Hearn filled five big sheets with all the information he could gather about Tampa, from facts about fleas to a glowing eulogy of the moon,—"seven times larger than your cold moon."

Following upon his translations of Gautier, Hearn busied himself with translations from Flaubert, and sent the manuscript of the proposed title-page and introduction to Mr. Watkin to set up, as he was superstitious about his "Dear Old Dad" bringing him luck. As usual he urged his friend to visit him, drawing in a letter of September 14, 1882, the following alluring pictures:

"In October we shall have exquisite weather—St. Martin's summer, the Creoles call it,—something like Indian summer North. Then I shall indeed hope to see you. No danger now of fever; and will have a nice healthy room for you. If you can't get away in October, wait till November,—nice and clear month generally, with orange-blossom smells. Raven wants to have a big talk. As for writing, don't write if it bothers you. I am sure you cannot have much time and must take care of your eyes. Perhaps some day we can both take things more easily, and a long rest by running streams, near mountain winds and in a climate like unto an eternal mountain springtime. Dream of voices of birds, whisper of leaves, milky quivering of stars, laughing of streams, odors of pine and of savage flowers, shadows of flying clouds, winds triumphantly free. Horrible cities! vile air! abominable noises! sickness! humdrum human machines! Let us strike our tents! move a little nearer to Nature!"

October 26, 1882, still writing about the promised visit of Mr. Watkin, he sent the following:

"MY DEAR OLD MAN: As the twig is bent, &c.—neither you nor I can now correct ourselves of habits. We are both old. [Hearn was thirty-two and Mr. Watkin fifty-nine.] I, for my part, feel ancient as the moon, and regret the departure of my youth. But I observe that all my best friends have the same habit. There's Charley Johnson,—wrote me twice in five years. There's the old newspaper coteries never write me at all. There is myself, just as bad as anybody. When somebody asked Théophile Gautier to write, he answered, 'Oh, ask a carpenter to plane planks just for fun!' It is a fact. Life's too short.... I was afraid for a while that Yellow Jack was trying to climb up this way from Pensacola; but I think all danger is now over. The weather feels chilly to us,—alligator-blooded and web-footed dwellers of the swamp (the Dismal Swamp): it will feel warm to you....

"Yes; I think a river trip down would be nicer for you, as it would include rest, good living, and a certain magical illusion of Southern beauties which bewitched me into making my dwelling-place among the frogs and bugs and the everlasting mosquitoes. 'Bugs' here mean every flying and crawling thing whereof the entomology is unknown to the people. The electric lights nightly murder centillions of them."

The letter is signed as usual with the drawing of a raven. As a novelty, the bird is looking at a steamer bearing over the side-wheel the name *Watkin*.

November 24, 1882, he wrote to Mr. Watkin, foreshadowing the book, "Stray Leaves from Strange Literatures," which was to bring him his first meed of praise from all sides. Again in this letter he somewhat despondently referred to his being a small man in a world where, according to his morbid views, big men won all the battles:

"I'm busy on a collection of Oriental legends,—Brahmanic, Buddhistic, Talmudic, Arabic, Chinese, and Polynesian,—which I hope to have ready in the spring. I think I can get Scribner or Osgood to bring it out.

"I think myself that life is worth living under the conditions you speak of; but they are very hard to obtain. I would be glad to try a new climate,—a new climate is a new life, a new youth. Here the problem of existence forever stares one in the face with eyes of iron. Independence is so hard to obtain,—the churches, the societies, the organizations, the cliques, the humbugs are all working against the man who tries to preserve independence of thought and action. Outside of these one cannot obtain a woman's society, and if obtained one is forever buried in the mediocrity to which she belongs.... My idea of perfect bliss would be ease and absolute quiet,—silence, dreams, tepidness,—great quaint rooms overlooking a street full of shadows and emptiness,—friends in the evening, a pipe, a little philosophy, wandering under the moon.... I am beginning to imagine that to be forever in the company of one woman would kill a man with ennui. And I feel that I am getting old—immemorially old,—older than the moon. I ought never to have been born in this century, I think sometimes, because I live forever in dreams of other centuries and other faiths and other ethics,—dreams rudely broken by the sound of cursing in the street below, cursing in seven different languages. I can't tell you much else about myself. I live in my books, and the smoke of my pipe, and ideas that nobody has any right expelling a good time in this world unless he be gifted with great physical strength and force of will. These give success. Little phantoms of men are blown about like down in the storms of the human struggle: they have not enough weight to keep them in place. And the Talmud says: 'There are three whose life is no life: the Sympathetic man, the Irascible, and the Melancholy.' But alas! the art by which the Sorceress of Colchis could recreate a body by cutting it up and boiling it in a pot is lost. Don't you think happiness is solely the result of perfect health under normal conditions of existence? I believe in the German philosopher who said that whether one had a billion dollars a day or only one dollar a week, it made no difference in regard to the amount of happiness a human brain was susceptible of. Still, it would be so nice to avoid the opposite by walling oneself up from the human species,—like the Cainites, whose cities were 'walled up to Heaven.'"

There now ensues in the correspondence, a silence extending over a period of nearly five years. These were busy years for Hearn. His position in the New Orleans newspaper world became a prominent one, and his translations of stories from the French, made for the papers by which he was employed, were so favorably received as to give him greater confidence in his own abilities.

Early in June of the year 1887 things began to take a turn for greater work for Hearn. His studies of the negroes and the Creoles of Louisiana had attracted the attention of the publishers, and he had received some rather tempting offers to do work for them. It was then that he left New Orleans, going to New York by way of Cincinnati. With all of his old shyness, his avoidance of mere acquaintances, and his love of the white-haired old gentleman, who alone in Cincinnati had understood him, Hearn spent his entire day in Cincinnati in chat at Watkin's printing office, which was then situated at 26 Longworth Street. It was there that Hearn saw once more the tall clock, whose peculiar ticking seemed to have fascinated him and to which references are made even in his few letters from Japan. After the day with Mr. Watkin, he went direct to New York, where he was the guest of his friend, Mr. H. E. Krehbiel, the well-known musical critic, who was then living at 438 West 57th Street. From there it was that Hearn wrote to his mentor the following confession of affection and gratitude:

"DEAR OLD MAN: A delightful trip brought me safe and sound to New York, where my dear friend Krehbiel was waiting to take me to his cosy home. I cannot tell you how much our little meeting delighted me, or how much I regretted to depart so soon, or how differently I regarded our old friendship from my old way of looking at it. I was too young, too foolish, and too selfish to know you as you are, when we used to be together. Ten years made little exterior change in me, but a great deal of heart-change; and I saw you as you are,—noble and true and frank and generous, and felt I loved you more than I ever did before; felt also how much I owed you, and will always owe you,—and understood how much allowance you had made for all my horrid, foolish ways when I used to be with you. Well, I am sure to see you again.' I am having one of the most delightful holidays here I ever had in my life; and I expect to stay a few weeks. If it were not for the terrible winters, I should like to live in New York. Some day I suppose I shall have to spend a good deal of my time here. The houses eleven stories high, that seem trying to climb into the moon,—the tremendous streets and roads,—the cascading thunder of the awful torrent of life,—the sense of wealth-force and mind-power that oppresses the stranger here,—all these form so colossal a contrast with the inert and warmly colored Southern life that I know not how to express my impression. I can only think that I have found superb material for a future story, in which the influence of New York on a Southern mind may be described. Well, new as these things may seem to me, they are, no doubt, old and uninteresting to you,—so that I shall not bore you with my impressions. I will look forward to our next meeting, when during a longer stay in Cin. I can tell you such little experiences of my trip as may please you. I want to get into that dear little shop of yours again. I dreamed of it the other night, and heard the ticking of the old clock like a man's feet treading on pavement far away; and I saw the Sphinx, with the mother and child in her arms, move her monstrous head, and observe: 'The sky in New York is grey!'

"When I woke up it *was* grey, and it remained grey until to-day. Even now it is not like our summer blue. It looks higher and paler and colder. We are nearer to God in the South, just as we are nearer to Death in that terrible and splendid heat of the Gulf Coast. When I write God, of course I mean only the World-Soul, the mighty and sweetest life of Nature, the great Blue Ghost, the Holy Ghost which fills planets and hearts with beauty.

"Believe me, Dear Old Dad,
"Affectionately, your son,
"LAFCADIO HEARN"

Below this is once more the familiar drawing of the raven.

From this time on the letters came at greater and greater intervals. There were only three more from America and then four from Japan. It was not that Hearn forgot his old friend or cared less for him. But he became busier, and with larger projects, newer aims, and a different life, there was less time in which to indulge himself in the active correspondence of former years. Between the New York group of letters and those from Japan is a gap. Letters on both sides had become a matter of years instead of weeks or months. Mr. Watkin, with the increasing weight of years on his shoulders and the increasing cares of a business that had begun to decline with the introduction of modern printing methods, found less time to write to his Raven.

Early in July, 1887, Hearn at last departed on that long-wished-for journey to the West Indies. A note, hastily scribbled to Mr. Watkin, told of the arrangements:

"DEAR OLD MAN: I leave on the *Barracouta* for Trinidad, Sunday, at daybreak. I have been travelling about a good deal, and have been silent only because so busy and so tired when the business was over. Your dear letter and your excellent little stamp both delighted me. I will let you hear from me soon again,—that is, as soon as I can get to a P. O.

"With affection, always your little Raven,
"LAFCADIO HEARN"

This promise of frequent letters was one he was not destined to keep. Once in the West Indies, he found himself so enthralled by its beauties, so busy putting on paper his impressions of what he was seeing and breathing and feeling, that it was not until he was once more in the United States that he found time to write.

September 21, 1887, he sent the following from Metuchen, New Jersey:

"DEAR OLD DAD: After three months or so in the West Indies and British Guiana, I am back again in the U. S. in first-rate health and spirits. I ought to have been able to write you, I thought, from Martinique; but the enormous and unexpected volume of work I had to do rendered it almost impossible to write anything except business letters to Harpers, and one or two necessary notes to friends looking after my affairs elsewhere. My conviction is that you and I would do well to spend our lives in the Antilles. All dreams of Paradise (even Mahomet's) are more than realized there by nature;—after returning, I find this world all colorless, all grey, and fearfully cold. I feel like an outcast from heaven. But it is no use trying to tell you anything about it in a letter. I wrote nearly three hundred pages of manuscript to the Harpers about it,—and I have not been able to say one thousandth part. I got two little orders for stamps for you at Martinique,— pencil stamps like the one you made for me. One is to be 'Plissonneau, fils;' the other, 'A. Testart.' Send bill to me, and stamps to A. Testart, St. Pierre, Martinique, French W. Indies. I hope to see you on my way South, dear old Dad.

"Believe me always,

"LAFCADIO HEARN"

In view of the terrible catastrophe at St. Pierre, it would be interesting to know whether Hearn's friends perished in that fury of fire and lava and hot ashes. Hearn's expectations about returning to New Orleans were not destined to be fulfilled. So successful had he been in his work for Harpers that, a week later than the date of the previous letter, he had the satisfaction of announcing that he was going back to what at that time seemed to him the most delightful region in the world. The opening of this letter is unique, in that it is the only one in which he is in the least ceremonious:

"H. WATKIN, ESQ., DEAR OLD DAD: I am going right back to the Tropics again, this time to stay. I have quit newspapering forever. Wish I could see you and chat with you before I go, but I cannot get a chance this time. My address will be care American Consul, St. Pierre, Martinique, Lesser Antilles. I may not be there all the time, but that will be my headquarters, and there letters will always reach me. To-day I am packing, rushing around breathlessly, preparing to go,—so that my letter must be brief. I did better with my venture than I ever expected; for I got for my work done seven hundred dollars, besides having secured material for much better work. You will hear of me in the *Harper's Magazine* this winter,—beginning about January and February. I shall be able hereafter to rest where I please; so that I shall have no trouble, when I get to New York again, in running to Cincinnati. Of course I don't want my little plans known yet,—because no one knows what might turn up; but these are the present prospers,—quite bright for me. I will write from Martinique or Guadeloupe, and try to coax you to go down there. Good-bye for a little while, with my best love to you.

"L. HEARN"

Again this promise of letters from the West Indies was destined to be broken. While lotus-eating, Hearn wrote few letters. He was most probably busy, amid the glow and color of the Antilles, studying the philosophical, scientific, and religious works which were destined so strongly to color his writings about Japan. He went to the latter country in 1890. In order that the reader may have a clear understanding of events, the facts in Hearn's Japanese career may be told in a few words. In 1890 and 1891 he served as English teacher in the ordinary middle school and the normal school of Matsue in Izumo. Next he was connected with the government school at Kumamoto. Then came newspaperwork at Kobe, and finally in 1896 he was honored by being made lecturer on English literature at the Imperial University of Tokio, which position he held until 1903, when he retired, owing to increasing trouble with his eyes, which had caused him anxiety all his life. He was contemplating a lecture trip in the United States, but ill health prevented. He died at his Tokio home September 26, 1904, and was buried September 29, with the Buddhist rites, the funeral service being held at the temple of Jito-in of Ichigaya. He now sleeps in the lonely old cemetery of Zōshigaya in the outskirts of the capital. Shortly after Hearn reached Japan Mr. Watkin obtained his address, and wrote him a letter telling how often he had thought of him and had expected to hear from him in the two years and more that had elapsed since their last letters. This brought a speedy reply,—a reply which showed that, so far as his feeling for the old English printer was concerned, there was little difference between the immature, ambition-stung youth of nineteen and the well-known, mature author of forty, who felt in some dim way that there amid this Oriental people he was destined to live and die. The reply to Mr. Watkin is from Yokohama, and, contrary to Hearn's previous rule, is actually dated,—April 25, 1890.

"DEAR OLD DAD: I was very happy to feel that your dear heart thought about me; I also have often found myself dreaming of you. I arrived here, by way of Canada and Vancouver, after passing some years in the West Indies. I think I shall stay here some years. I have not been getting rich,— quite the contrary; but I am at least preparing a foundation for ultimate independence,—if I keep my health. It is very good now, but I have many grey hairs, and I shall be next June forty years old.

"I trust to make enough in a year or two to realize my dream of a home in the West Indies; if I succeed, I must try to coax you to come along, and dream life away quietly where all is sun and beauty. But no one ever lived who seemed more a creature of circumstances than I; I drift with various forces in the direction of least resistance,—resolve to love nothing, and love always too much for my own peace of mind,—places, things, and persons,—and lo! presto! everything is swept away, and becomes a dream,—like life itself.

"Perhaps there will be a great awakening; and each will cease to be an Ego, but an All, and will know the divinity of Man by seeing, as the veil falls, himself in each and all.

"Here I am in the land of dreams,—surrounded by strange Gods. I seem to have known and loved them before somewhere: I burn incense before them. I pass much of my time in the temples, trying to see into the heart of this mysterious people. In order to do so I have to blend with them and become a part of them. It is not easy. But I hope to learn the language; and if I do not, in spite of myself, settle here, you will see me again. If you do not, I shall be under big trees in some old Buddhist cemetery, with six laths above me, inscribed with prayers in an unknown tongue, and a queerly carved monument typifying those five elements into which we are supposed to melt away. I trust all is well with you, dear old Dad. Write me when it will not pain your eyes. Tell me all you can about yourself. Be sure that I always remember you; and that my love goes to you.

"LAFCADIO HEARN

"I could tell you so much to make you laugh if you were here; and to hear you laugh again would make me very happy."

An interval of over four years now occurred before Hearn wrote once more to Cincinnati. Some very decided changes had taken place in his life. He had wedded a Japanese woman, he had a son, and he was reputed to have become a Buddhist. He had been successful with his literary work, his essays on things Japanese being among the most noteworthy and popular articles in the *Atlantic Monthly*. It was at this period, when Mr. Watkin thought his friend was most happy, that he received a long reply from Japan in response to a joint letter sent by the old gentleman and his daughter, Miss Effie Watkin. It is a singular thing that it was not until this time that Hearn ever mentioned Mr. Watkin's wife and daughter. He had in truth been few times in their presence. Mrs. Watkin, a woman of strong common sense, had found the foolish superstitions of the young lad hard to bear, and he had accordingly, when in Cincinnati, confined his particular friendship to the husband and father. The letter from Hearn rather surprised its recipient by reason of its despondency. It had much of the old gloomy cast of thought. For this there were two potent reasons. One was his worry over his son's future. The other was his worry over that Japan he had learned to love so well. He felt doubtful about the outcome of the war with China,—the letter was written in September, 1894,—and troubles for the Mikado's empire always made him a little sad. Singularly enough, the same feeling can be traced very clearly in his book, "Japan, An Attempt at Interpretation," written in the first months of the struggle with Russia.

One other word of introductory comment is necessary. His seeming depreciation of his own essays was only the reflection of his general gloomy viewpoint at the time the letter was written. Hearn was dwelling at the time at Kumamoto.

"Dear Old Dad: It delighted me to get that kindest double letter from yourself and sweet-hearted little daughter,—or rather delighted us. My wife speaks no English, but I translated it for her. She will send a letter in Japanese, which Miss Effie will not be able to read, but which she will keep as a curiosity perhaps. Our love to you both.

"How often I have thought of you, and wondered about you, and wished I could pass with you more of the old-fashioned evenings, reading ancient volumes of the *Atlantic Monthly*,—so much better a magazine in those days than in these, when I am regularly advertised as one of its contributors.

"I often wonder now at your infinite patience with the extraordinary, superhuman foolishness and wickedness of the worst pet you ever had in your life. When I think of all the naughty, mean, absurd, detestable things I did to vex you and to scandalize you, I can't for the life of me understand why you did n't want to kill me,—as a sacrifice to the Gods. What an idiot I was!—and how could you be so good?—and why do men change so? I think of my old self as of something which ought not to have been allowed to exist on the face of the earth,—and yet, in my present self, I sometimes feel ghostly reminders that the old self was very real indeed. Well, I wish I were near you to love you and make up for all old troubles.

"I have a son. He is my torment and my pride. He is not like me or his mother. He has chestnut hair and blue eyes, and is enormously strong,— the old Gothic blood came out uppermost. I am, of course, very anxious about him. He *can't* become a Japanese,—his soul is all English, and his looks. I must educate him abroad. Head all above the ears,—promises to be intelligent. I shall never have another child. I feel too heavily the tremendous responsibility of the thing. But the boy is there,—intensely alive; and I must devote the rest of my existence to him. One thing I hope for is that he will never be capable of doing such foolish things as his daddy used to do. His name is Kaji-we or Ka-jio. He does not cry, and has a tremendous capacity for growing. And he gives me the greatest variety of anxiety about his future.

"When you hear that I have been able to save between thirty-five hundred and four thousand dollars, you will not think I have made no progress. But I have put all, or all that I could reasonably do, in my wife's name. The future looks very black. The reaction against foreign influence is strong; and I feel more and more every day that I shall have to leave Japan eventually, at least for some years. When I first met you I was—nineteen. I am now forty-four! Well, I suppose I must have lots more trouble before I go to Nirvana.

"Effie says you do not see my writings. My book will be out by the time you get this letter,—that is, my first book on Japan.[1] Effie can read bits of it to you. And I figure in the *Atlantic* every few months. Cheap fame;—the amazing fortune I once expected does n't turn up at all. I have been obliged to learn the fact that I am not a genius, and that I must be content with the crumbs from the table of Dives.

"But this is all Egotism. I am guilty of it only because you asked for a small quantity. About yourself and all who love you my letter rather ought to be. Speak always well of me to John Chamberlain [a journalist]. I liked him well. Do you remember the long walks over the Ohio, in the evening, among the fireflies and grasshoppers, to hear lectures upon spiritual things? If I were near you now, I could saturate you with Oriental spiritualism,—Buddhism,—everything you would like, but after a totally novel fashion. When one has lived alone five years in a Buddhist atmosphere, one naturally becomes penetrated by the thoughts that hover in it; my whole thinking, I must acknowledge, has been changed, in spite of my long studies of Spencer and of Schopenhauer. I do not mean that I am a Buddhist, but I mean that the inherited ancestral feelings about the universe—the Occidental ideas every Englishman has—have been totally transformed.

"There is yet no fixity, however: the changes continue,—and I really do not know how I shall feel about the universe later on. What a pity that Western education and Western ideas only corrupt and spoil the Japanese,—and that the Japanese peasant is now superior to the Japanese noble!

"You have heard of the war. The Japanese are a fighting race; and I think they will win all the battles. But to conquer a Chinese army is not the same thing as to conquer the Chinese government. The war makes us all uneasy. Japan's weakness is financial. A country where it costs a dollar a month to live, and where the population is only forty million, is not really strong enough for such an enormous job. Our hope is that science and rapidity of movement may compensate for smallness of resources.

"I am almost sure I shall have to seek America again. If that happens, I shall see you or die. All now is doubt and confusion. But in this little house all is love to you. We have your picture;... we all know you, as if you were an old acquaintance.

"I wish we could be together somewhere for a pleasant evening chat, hearing in the intervals the office clock, like the sound of a long-legged walker. I wish we could talk over all the hopes and dreams of ideal societies, and the reasons of the failure to realize them. I wish I could tell you about the ideas of Western civilization which are produced by a long sojourn in the Orient. How pleasant to take country walks again! that is, if there be any country left around Cincinnati. How pleasant to read to you strange stories and theories from the Far East! Still, I have become so accustomed to Japanese life that a return to Western ways would not be altogether easy at first. What a pity I did not reach Japan ten years sooner!

"Tell me, if you write again, all pleasant news about old friends. Love to you always, and believe me ever,

"Your extremely bad and ungrateful

"Grey-headed boy,

"LAFCADIO HEARN"

[1] *Glimpses of Unfamiliar Japan.*

Shortly after this long letter came the one written by Hearn's Japanese wife, accompanied by this note:

"DEAR MISS EFFIE: Here is my wife's answer to your most kind letter. She thanks you very much for writing,—says that she knows your papa well, by looking at his photograph, and by hearing me talk of him; she apologizes for not being able to write or speak English; she hopes to see you some day, and to be shown by you some of the wonders of the Western world, about which she knows nothing; she tells you about our little son; and finally says that if she ever comes to America she will bring you some curious memento from Japan. It is all written in the old style of high Japanese courtesy, in which your letter is called 'jewel-pen letter.' Best regards and kindest love for your papa. We are going to leave Kumamoto. Will write again soon.

"LAFCADIO HEARN"

In 1895 an accident befell Mr. Watkin, and, upon his request, Mrs. Watkin wrote a letter to the distant friend. Mrs. Watkin was rather timid about it and was dubious about receiving a reply. However, despite this feeling, she enclosed some little verses of hers upon a spiritual theme. In a short time she received the following reply:

"*Kobe;—shimoyamatedori, Shichome*

"7 *Feb.* 28, 1895

"DEAR MRS. WATKIN: Your kind, sweet letter reached me by last American mail, and gave me all the pleasure you could have desired. But why have you even dreamed of apologizing for writing to me, who love you all, and for whom everything is comprehensible even if not wholly comprehended? All love and good wishes to you. I received the little poem, and liked it. Those mysteries in which you appear to be interested are scarcely mysteries in the Far East: the immaterial world counts here for more than the visible. Perhaps some day I may suddenly drop in upon you all, and talk ghostliness to you,—a new ghostliness, which you may like. Some hints of it appear in a little book of mine, to be issued about the time this letter reaches you,— 'Out of the East.'

"I really think I may see you and my dear old Dad again. I may be obliged erelong to return, at least temporarily, to America, to make some money, though my home must be in Japan till my boy grows up a little. He seems to be very strong and bright, and queerly enough he is fair. I have two souls now, which is troublesome; for his every word and cry stirs strange ripples in my own life, and the freedom of being responsible only for oneself is over forever for me. Whether this be for the worse or the better in the eternal order of things, the Gods must decide.

"I should like to see your new home. The other one was very cosy; but perhaps this is even better. What I also want to see is No. *16* Longworth Street, and to hear the ticking of the old clock that used to sound like the steps of a long-legged man walking on pavement. Effie wrote me a dear, pretty letter. Thank her for me. It is just about seven years now since I saw Dad. I suppose he looks now more like Homer than ever. .1 have become somewhat grey, and have crow's-feet around my eyes. Also I have become fat, and disinclined for violent exercise. In other words, I'm getting down the shady side of the hill,—and the horizon before me is already darkening, and the winds blowing out of it, cold. And I am not in the least concerned about the enigmas,—except that I wonder what my boy will do if I don't live to be nearly as old as Dad. Ever with all affectionate regards to him and yourself and Effie,

"Lafcadio Hearn"

In 1896 Mr. Watkin, partially recovered from his injuries, wrote Hearn a letter, and received a last one from him,—a reply in which the writer finally placed the seal upon the finest friendship in his history. Unlike some of his other attempts at prophecy, Hearn's predictions in this last letter failed to come true. He never saw his old friend again, and the old gentleman, at the age of eighty-two, now occupies a room in the Old Men's Home in Cincinnati, counting among his chief treasures the letters which have been here presented.

"*Kobe*
"*Nakayamatedori*
"*7-chome*
"*Bangai* 16
"*May* 23,'96

"Dear Old Dad: How nice to get so dear a letter from you! I know the cost to you of writing it, and my dear old father must not imagine that I do not understand why he cannot write often. With his little grey boy it is much the same now: he finds it hard to write letters, and he has very few correspondents. Why, indeed, should he have many? True men are few; and the autograph-hunters, and the scheming class of small publishers, and the people, who want gratis information about commercial matters in Japan are not considered by him as correspondents. They never get any answers. I have two or three dear friends in this world: is not that enough?—you being oldest and dearest. To feel that one has them is much.

"But I must ask many pardons. I fear Miss Effie will not forgive me for not acknowledging ere now the receipt of a photograph, which surprised as much as it pleased me. To think of the little girl having so developed into the fine serious woman! How old it makes me feel! for I remember Miss Effie when she was so little. Please ask her to forgive me. I was away when the photograph came (in Kyoto), and when I returned, lazily put off writing from day to day. There was, however, some excuse for my laziness. I have been very sick with inflammation of the lungs, and am getting well very slowly. But all danger is practically over.

"I see from the kind letter of protest bearing your initials that the idealism which makes love has never gone out of your heart when you think of me. It is all much more real than any materialism; see, you always predicted that I should be able to do something, while extremely practical, materialistic people predicted that I should end in jail or at the termination of a rope. And your prediction seems to have been wiser,—for at last, at last I am attracting a little attention in England.... Also I see (what I did not know before) that some people have been writing horrid things about me. I expected it, sooner or later, as I have been an open enemy of the missionaries; and, besides, the least success in this world must be atoned for. The price is heavy. Those who ignore you when you are nobody find it necessary to hate you when you disappoint their expectations. But if I keep my health I need not care very much. The incident only brought out some of the honey in dear old Dad's heart.

"You ask about my boy. I can best respond by sending his last photo,— nearly three years old now. If I can educate him in France or Italy, it would be better for him, I think. He is very sensitive; and I am afraid of American or English school training for him. I only pray the Gods will spare me till he is eighteen or twenty. I am watching to see what he will develop; if he have any natural gift, I shall try to cultivate only that gift. Ornamental education is a wicked, farcical waste of time. It left me incapacitated to do anything; and I still feel the sorrow of the sin of having dissipated ten years in Latin and Greek, and stuff,... when a knowledge of some one practical thing, and of a modern language or two, would have been of so much service. As it is, I am only self-taught; for everything I learned in school I have since had to unlearn. You helped me with some of the unlearning, dear old Dad!

"I really expect to see you. You are only seventy-two, and hale, and I trust you have long years before you, and that we shall meet. About the business depression, I hear that it is passing and that 'flush times' are in store for the West. This, I trust, will be. Oh, no! I shall not have to look for you 'in the old men's home,'—no, I shall see you in your own home,—and talk queer talk to you.

"For the time being (indeed, for two years) I have lived altogether by literary work, without breaking my little reserves, and it is likely that better things are in store for me. I am anxious for success,—for the boy's sake above all. To have the future of others to make—to feel the responsibilities—certainly changes the face of life. I am always frightened, of course; but I work and hope. That is the best, is it not? Remember me to all kind friends. Ask Effie to forgive my rude silence, and all yours to believe my love and constant remembrance.

"LAFCADIO HEARN

"I am a Japanese citizen now (Y. Koizumi),—adopted into the family of my wife. This settles all legal question as to property as well as marriage under Japanese law; and if I die, the Consul can't touch anything belonging to my people."

The rest is silence.

Letters to a Lady

Herewith are presented letters that were the outgrowth of a friendship that probably meant a great deal to Lafcadio Hearn at the time. In speaking of them, one inevitably thinks of Prosper Mérimée's "Lettres à une inconnue." The later missives, too, must for years to come remain "letters to an unknown,"—unknown to all save a few persons. It was only recently that the natural course of events made it at all possible to include them in this collection. Even now the ban of silence is placed on many things we would like to know.

The letters were written during the memorable year 1876, marked by exciting political conventions and an even more exciting national election, and finally by the great Centennial Exposition. At this time Hearn was in his twenty-sixth year. He had been in the United States for nearly six years, and was at the time employed as a reporter on Mr. Murat Halstead's Cincinnati *Commercial.* Although he did not like this country and was at this time dreaming of returning some day to Europe, he had been trying for years to make a thoroughly competent newspaper reporter of himself. However, we gather from remarks in his letters that he was still regarded as only a minor member of the staff.

Among men his chief friend remained Mr. Watkin. If he had any friends among young women, he has left no record of them. He seems to have been more or less solitary always. He is constantly telling of his constraint in social gatherings, of his inability to appear otherwise than cold to those around him. Life was indeed to him always a curious carnival, in which one must be careful to keep on the mask, to guard the tongue lest one say something redounding to one's injury or discredit.

With such characteristics, we are therefore at a loss to learn how his intimacy with the unknown began. It may have had its origin when some assignment in the line of newspaper duty took him to her home. One fancies the unknown must have had a keen eye for character and ability to discern anything unusual, anything love-worthy, in the ill-dressed, somewhat ill-featured, shy, timid, little youth Hearn was at that time. It had not heretofore been his good fortune to attract. However that may be, the established fact of the friendship remains.

The identity of the unknown is a secret. We are told that she was a woman of culture and refinement; that she was possessed of some wealth; and, finally, that she was many years older than Hearn.

Mérimée has been referred to. The reference is forced upon us by Hearn himself. He mentions those famous "Lettres," and says he feels toward his "Dear Lady" as Mérimée did toward his "inconnue." The comparison is not exact. Indeed, it is rather a case of contrast. Like Mérimée, Hearn's motto seems to have been, with very rare exceptions, "Remember to distrust;" but, unlike Mérimée, Hearn was not a man of wealth and prominence and influence in his native land; unlike Mérimée, Hearn had not had all the advantages wealth and culture can give; unlike Mérimée, he had known, and was still destined to know, hard and bitter years.

With Mérimée, the French stylist *par excellence*, impersonality was a passion. His was an impersonality that was broken down only in the famous "Lettres." Hearn, on the other hand, could not help injecting much of himself into his books. Nor does the contrast end there.

"For her first thoughts," as Walter Pater well says of the "Lettres" and the author's attitude toward the woman in the case, "Mérimée is always pleading, but always complaining that he gets only her second thoughts,— the thoughts, that is, of a reserved, self-limiting nature."

In the present collection of letters, the rôles are reversed. We gather from the letters that it was Hearn who never let himself go, who always kept himself under cautious restraint, and that it was the woman who resented these second thoughts, these promptings of careful meditations rather than of fresh, warm impulses.

In Mérimée the ardent lover alternated with the severe critic. He quarrelled with the unknown and then had reconciliations, until at last the old love passed away into a form of calm friendship. In the meantime he packed his letters with keen criticisms of books, society, politics, archæology, noted people,—everything that interested a citizen of the world.

In Hearn we have the lonely little egotist, writing mainly about himself. In his appreciation of a woman's friendship and his pride in her cordial admiration, he expands and reveals some part of his own thoughts, beliefs, studies. For the rest, the connection, on his side at least, seems to have been one of platonic friendship. The lady was more or less existing, Hearn being constantly occupied in explaining away what she was quick to fancy were slights.

She would seem to have been even more sensitive than he. To speak plainly, too, there is a note of evasion in his letters; despite his appreciation of her, he seems to have seized upon his newspaper work as an excuse for preventing their friendship becoming something more intimate. He kept things—at least in his letters—upon a very formal plane. He was to the recipient, one fancies, provokingly distant in his "Dear Lady" form of address. There was an ominous sign in the constant reference to letters returned or unopened. Indeed, there finally came the breach that in the nature of things was inevitable, and then all his letters were returned to him.

The young man did not destroy them. Shortly afterwards he departed for the South. It is not a little strange that in all the years in New Orleans that followed—lean years and fat, years of bitter poverty and of comparative prosperity—Hearn preserved this batch of letters intact. When nearing the age of forty and close to that period when he was to sail for Japan, the more or less matured man passed judgment upon the letters of his youth, found them good, and placed them in the keeping of his friend. He told Mr. Watkin to do with the faded missives what he deemed best. In some fashion he would seem to have felt that he was yet destined to accomplish something in the world of literature, and to have proudly thought that some day even these boyish screeds would be eagerly read.

As for these letters, as with most of Hearn's missives, they were for the most part undated,—written hurriedly on any kind of paper, often on mere scraps.

He places himself before us as the "Oriental by birth and half by blood;" as a lad destined for Catholicism, and, instead of that, savagely attacking the religion of his mother. We have hints of the hard measure the world had dealt him and how he felt like a barbarian beyond the pale of polite society. He confesses himself ill at ease among the cultivated classes, and we dimly feel that there were in those years, before he came to Cincinnati, days so bitter that they left a permanent mark. Without religious faith, going to the boyish extreme of lightly attacking Christianity, he imagined himself ready to become a sort of æsthetic pagan, worshipping Venus and the other gods of the antique world. As antagonistic to accepted pulpit teaching, he read Darwin, and pompously and not a little solemnly announced, "I accept Darwin fully."

Perhaps no inconsiderable portion of this paganism was caused by his youthful worship of Swinburne. All young men in the late sixties and early seventies, with an ear for verbal music and magic, were swearing allegiance to the bard of the famous "Poems and Ballads." Indeed, one feels that Hearn would have been a poet himself, had he but been gifted with the faculty of rhyme. Much of the other equipment of the poet was his in abundant measure,—the love of beauty, the love of lovely words, the joy in the manifold things of nature and art.

Speaking of Swinburne brings us to his reading, and we catch a glimpse of that little shelf of treasured books,—Balzacand Gautier and Rabelais in the French; Poe, to be sure; and—strange choice—the poems of Mr. Thomas Bailey Aldrich.

In these "Letters to a Lady" there is comparatively little discussion of literary subjects, save the mention of the fact that he is reading, always reading. Of literary criticism there is but little. In one letter, indeed, we do get a reference to the character of the Sultana of Aldrich's "Cloth of Gold," but this is a moral rather than a literary discussion. The sign that he was ranging far afield among other men's works, and also the hint of the writer that was to be, is given in little sentences dropped half unconsciously here and there,—sentences that to the student of Hearn's letters seem to be characteristic of his ways of thought, as when he says, "Somehow the ghosts of the letters I write by night laugh in my face by day;" or when he speaks of his horror of crowds and compares it to the terror of the desert camel being urged toward the white walls and shining minarets of the city beyond the desert; or when, curiously enough, he speaks of himself as seeming like a lizard in the July sun, a very similar turn of thought having been employed by Flaubert in one of his letters, which Hearn had probably never read, even though he did once plan a translation from that author.

It is only necessary in conclusion to call attention to one more letter in this section. As a matter of plain prose it would seem that the lady had complained of the coldness and the dubious tone of some of Hearn's letters and had returned them to him. In response he wrote to her a fable of a Sultan and a neighboring Sultana. He told how the Sultana complained of the Sultan's messengers, and how the Sultan committed them to death by fire. The lady was supposed, from this pretty fable, to draw the conclusion that Hearn's letters had been destroyed by their author. From the collection herewith appended, it can be seen that the fabulist availed himself of poetic license.

I

DEAR FRIEND: Your last kind letter makes me in some sort ashamed of my diffidence and coldness. Yet you must be aware how peculiarly I feel myself situated,—constrained, watched everywhere by a hundred eyes that know me, hemmed in with conventionalities of which I only know the value sufficiently to have my nerves on a perpetual strain through fear of breaking them. I am not by nature cold,—quite the reverse, indeed, as many a bitter experience taught me; and I beg you to attribute my manner rather to overcaution than to indifference to the feelings of others. Why, do not we all wear masks in this great carnival mummery of life, in which we all dance and smile disguisedly, until the midnight of our allotted pleasure time comes; and the King-Skeleton commands, "Masks off—show your skulls"? I am afraid you do not understand [me]; or rather, I feel sure you do not wholly,—for you have had little opportunity. You have only seen me on my best behavior; perhaps you might think less of me under other circumstances, but never think me a chilly phantom, though you may occasionally see me only as the Shadow of that which I really am. Have I been rude? Try to forgive my rudeness. It was involuntary.... I think I understood your letters; and I did not form any opinion therefrom, I feel sure, which you would not have liked. I wish I could be less strained and conventional in company. Will try my best to do better. Sincerely,

L. HEARN

II

DEAR FRIEND AND LADY (if I may so call you): Do not suppose that when I delay answering one of your kind letters, the tardiness is attributable to neglect: or forgetfulness or inappreciation of your favor. I thoroughly feel—and feel keenly—every kind word or thought you have expressed or felt forme; I have never rendered you, it is true, a single compliment worthy of those I have received,—but only because I was sure that you understood my feelings better than if I had expressed them; I never write altogether as I think, partly because I am not naturally demonstrative, and while capable of more than ordinary sensitive feeling, I have a kind of reluctance to take off what I might term my little mask. Don't hesitate to scold me, as you threaten, should you think I deserve it....

I have been busy all day among noisy crowds of enthusiastic Catholics; and I shudder at the thought of entering a crowd at all times, just as the desert camel shudders when his driver urges him toward the white walls and the shining minarets of a city sparkling beyond the verge of the silent yellow waste. Consequently I was not able to write till late; and even now I am not in a good writing humor. One's skull becomes peopled with Dreams and Fantastic Things just before daybreak; and if you notice aught foolish or absurd in these lines, please attribute them to that weird influence which comes on us all—

"in the dead vast and middle of the night."

I must make one more visit to the Central Police Station ere cockcrow,— poetically speaking.

Sincerely,

LAF. HEARN

III

Cincinnati, Thursday, 27, 1876

DEAR LADY: I return by mail the very interesting letters which you kindly left for my perusal; also, the list of Mr.'s collection, whereof I have taken a copy. The other collectors are so slow in preparing their lists that I fear I shall not be able to publish a full account of their contributions to the

World's Exposition for several days yet.... I am very thankful for your assistance in obtaining information regarding these things.

As an English subject, and one who feels a kind of home interest in European news, you may feel assured that the letters from beyond the "great water" interested me extremely.

The author gives a pleasant, realistic, and entertaining picture of the brilliant social affair whereof her letter treats; and her account would have done credit to most foreign newspaper correspondents, speaking from a journalistic point of view....

Believe me very respectfully yours,

L. HEARN

IV

There is a fragment in which is taken up the matter of invitations he has refused. It is chiefly interesting because of his expressed desire to return to Europe:

"I daily receive and pay no attention whatever to other invitations, because I know my presence is only desired for journalistic favors; but with you I regret to be unable to accept them quite as much as you could. In speaking of impulses, I refer merely to sudden actions without preparation,—such as your first note of yesterday; or your action on fancying that I had been talking too much; or your becoming vexed at me for what I could not help. You ought to know that I would do anything in my power to please you or to accommodate you....

"Let me also take this opportunity of thanking you for those books again. I have been very much fascinated by one of them and have not only read but re-read it. It is seemingly by some strange fatuity that your little invitations have latterly fallen on busy days. Last week it was all work; and this week I have had a very easy time of it. You looked at me yesterday as if I had done you some injury, and you hated to see me. If you go to Europe, my best wishes go with you. I hope to return there, and leave this country forever some day in the remote future.

"Do not be offended at my letter.

"L. H."

V

In a letter dated "Thursday p. m., 1876" we find him apologizing for some breach of etiquette. He then, as usual, complains of the newspaper man's lot:

"This afternoon I received your kind note. One of the misfortunes of a journalistic existence is the inability of a newspaper man to fulfil an appointment, meet an engagement, or definitely accept an invitation not immediately connected with his round of regular duty, as he may at any moment be ordered to the most outlandish places in the pursuit of news. I think, however, that I may safely accept your kind invitation to dine with you on Sunday at one o'clock p. m., and also to ride out to Avondale. Nothing could give me greater pleasure; the more so as Sunday is an inordinately dull day in the newspaper sphere. I will certainly be on hand unless something very extraordinary should intervene to prevent; and in such event I shall endeavor to inform you beforehand, so as not to cause you any trouble.

"I remain, dear Lady,

"Very respectfully,

"L. HEARN"

VI

Cincinnati, Friday, 1876 DEAR LADY: I very much regret that I should have inadvertently worded my last note in so clumsy a manner as to make it appear that in accepting your kind invitation I was prospectively interested in nothing but "items" and thankful only for the opportunity of obtaining news. In mentioning that I was especially glad to accept your invitation on Sunday, "as it is an especially dull day for news," I simply meant that I would find more leisure time on Sunday than upon any other day in the week; and would thus feel more pleasure in making a call without being worried by office business. I hope you will therefore consider my rudeness the result of hurried writing and clumsy phraseology rather than of deliberate ignorance.

If it be agreeable to you, I will call upon you at 1 p. m. on Sunday as per invitation. I cannot definitely say, however, what I could do in the way of writing an account of other collections than what have already been spoken of, inasmuch as I am, you know, only a reporter in the office, and subject to orders from the City Editor.

As I have not written any letters except of a business character for several years, please to excuse any apparent lack of courtesy in my note. I am apt to say something malapropos without intending. I remain,

Very respectfully yours,

LAFCADIO HEARN

VII

DEAR LADY: Excuse my tardiness in replying to your kind and, may I say, too complimentary letter; for I scarcely deserve the courteous interest you have expressed in regard to myself. Also let me assure you that you are very much mistaken in fancying that I am so used to all kinds of people as to feel no pleasure in such introductions as that of Sunday evening. The fact is that I was very much pleased; but am so poor a hand at compliments that I feared even to express to Miss —— the pleasure I felt in her songs and playing, to wish you many happy returns of your birthday, or to hint how well I enjoyed the conversation of your lady sister. I have not visited out since I was sixteen,—nine years ago; have led a very hard and extraordinary life previous to my connection with the press,—became a species of clumsy barbarian,—and in short for various reasons considered myself ostracized, tabooed, outlawed. These facts should be sufficient to explain to you that I am not used to all sorts of people,—not to the cultivated class of people at all, and feel all the greater pleasure in such a visit as that referred to....

I have not had time yet to conclude the entertaining volume of travel you kindly sent me, but have read sufficient to interest me extremely. I find a vast number of novel and hitherto unpublished facts,—the results of more than ordinarily keen observation in the work. If I were reviewing the book, I might feel inclined to take issue with the author in respect to his views concerning the work of the missionaries in Tahiti,—who have been, you know, most severely criticised by radically minded observers; but the writer's pictures are clearly defined, realistic, and powerfully drawn. I must not waste your time, however, with further gossip just now.

Believe me, dear Lady,

Very respectfully yours,

L. HEARN

VIII

DEAR LADY: I am not so insusceptible to such pretty flattery as yours, even though I think it undeserved, as to feel otherwise than pleased. Of course I am vain enough to be gratified at anything good said of me by you or your friends. In regard to enjoying music and flowers, I would only say that I love everything beautiful, and can only look at the social, ethical, or natural world with the eyes of a pagan rather than a Christian, revering the heathen philosophy of æsthetic sense; and surely so must all who truly love the antique loveliness of the Antique World, which deified all fair things and worshipped only those beauties of form and sense whereof it brought forth the highest types. But to speak truly, I am afraid of parties; one's nerves are ever on a painful strain in the effort to be agreeable, in the fear of doing something gauche, and in the awful perplexity of searching for

compliments which must fall on the ear as vapid and commonplace,—
vanity and vexation of spirit. Indeed, I much enjoyed the little party the
other night, because it was a home circle; and I did not feel as though
people were scrutinizing my face, my manners, my dress, or criticising my
words with severe mental criticism, or making the awful discovery that I
"had hands" and did not know what to do with them.

I did not tell you when my vacation should commence, because I did not
know myself; indeed, I do not yet know. Our vacations generally
commence about June, when each one in turn takes a couple or three
weeks' travel and rest; but as I am the youngest and freshest (in the sense of
inexperience) of the staff, I suppose I will have to wait my turn until the
others have decided. Some like to escape the hot weather. I love hot
weather,—the hotter the better. I feel always like a lizard in the July sun;
and when the juice of the poison plants is thickest and the venomous
reptiles most active, then I, too, feel life most enjoyable, as "Elsie Venner"
did. Therefore I may have to wait for my vacation till the golden autumn
cometh; but I will endeavor to get away so soon as I can, and will let you
know just so soon as I know myself.

Very respectfully yours, dear Lady,

LAFCADIO HEARN

IX

Cincinnati, May 9, 1876

DEAR LADY: I am at once gratified and surprised to find that my little
article should have given you so much pleasure. Had I not been very busy
with a mass of matter-of-fact work last evening, I should have done better
justice to Mr.——'s splendid collection. That was a very unfortunate
mistake of mine in regard to his name, but I shall try to correct it.

In regard to mentioning Mr.——'s name,

I desire to say to you, in strict confidence, that I purposely omitted it for
prudential reasons. Newspapers are very jealous of their employés in the
matter of giving compliments; and I feared that further mention just at this
time might render it all the more difficult for me to do you a reportorial
kindness on some future occasion. This may seem odd; but one outside the
newspaper circle can have no idea how particular newspaper proprietors
are.

With regard to my article, dear Lady, I would say, in reply to your kind
query, that you are welcome to use it as you please. I only regret the lack of
time to have improved it before it appeared in the *Commercial.* My love for

things Oriental need not surprise you, as I happen to be an Oriental by birth and half by blood.

I cannot definitely answer you in regard to the prospective country visit, so courteously proposed, until I see you again or hear from you. I fear I shall have to postpone the pleasure until the regular reporters' vacation time,— that is, if it should necessitate absence from duty for any considerable length of time. However, you can explain further when I again have the pleasure of seeing you; and if I can possibly get away, I will be only too glad of so pleasant a holiday.

Very respectfully and gratefully,

L. HEARN

X

DEAR LADY: If I disappointed you last evening, be sure that I myself was much more disappointed, especially as I had to pass within a stone's throw of your house without going in. I believe that if you only knew how frightfully busy we all are, you would have postponed the invitation until next week, when I shall have some leisure and hope to see you. I had expected up to the last moment to be able to call, if only for an hour; but a sudden appointment put it out of my power. The convention is keeping us all as busy as men can be.

I see you returned my letter. I know it was not a satisfactory one. Somehow the ghosts of the letters I write by night laugh in my face by day. I either talk too freely or write too hurriedly. I will not certainly give your books away, for I prize them highly and am delighted with them. I had thought they were only lent. They now nestle on my book-shelf along with a copy of Balzac's "Contes Drolatiques," illustrated by Doré, Gautier's most Pre-Raphael and wickedest work, Swinburne, Edgar Poe, Rabelais, Aldrich, and some other odd books which form my library. I generally read a little before going to bed.

I hope to visit your farm indeed, but the journalist is a creature who sells himself for a salary. He is a slave to his master, and must await the course of events.

No; you must not pity me or feel sorry for me. What would you do if I were to write you some of my up-and-down experiences and absurdities? And you cannot be of service to me except I were suddenly to lose everything and not know where to turn. Now I am doing very well, and would be doing better but for an escapade....

Of course I will write you in P—; I should like nothing better, feeling towards you like Prosper Mérimée to his "inconnue." I wish I could make my letters equally interesting.

I do not think that I am unfortunate in life, and yet I have done everything to make me so. If you only knew some of my follies, you would cease perhaps to like me. Some day I will confide some of my oddities to you. But don't think me unfortunate because I am a skeptic.

Skepticism is hereditary on my father's side. My mother, a Greek woman, was rather reverential; she believed in the Oriental Catholicism,—the Byzantine fashion of Christianity which produced such hideous madonnas and idiotic-looking saints in stained glass. I think being skeptical enables one to enjoy life better,—to live like the ancients without thought of the Shadow of Death. I was once a Catholic,—at least, my guardians tried to make me so, but only succeeded in making me dream of all priests as monsters and hypocrites, of nuns as goblins in black robes, of religion as epidemic insanity, useful only in inculcating ethics in coarse minds by main force. Afterwards it often delighted me to force a controversy upon some priest, deny his basis of belief, and find him startled to discover that he could not attempt to establish it logically.

You say, "What else is there" but faith to make life pleasant? Why, the majority of things that faith despises. I fancy if one will only try to analyze the amount of comfort derived from Christianity by himself, he will find the candid answer. Whence come all our arts, our loves, our luxuries, our best literature, our sense of manhood to do and dare, our reverence or respect: for Woman, our sense of beauty, our sense of humanity? Never from Christianity. From the antique faiths, the dead civilizations, the lost Greece and Rome, the warrior-creed of Scandinavia, the Viking's manhood and reverence for woman,—his creator and goddess. Yet all faiths surely have their ends in shaping and perfecting this electrical machine of the human mind, and preparing the field of humanity for a wider harvest of future generations, long after the worms, fed from our own lives, have ceased to writhe about us, as the serpents writhe among the grinning masks of stone on the columns of Persepolis.

How you must be bored by so long a letter!

[*The letter is signed by a drawing of the raven, familiar in the letters to Mr. Watkin.*]

XI

DEAR LADY: There once lived an Eastern Sultan who reigned over a city fairer than far Samarcand. He dwelt in a gorgeous palace of the most bizarre and fantastically beautiful Saracenic design,—columns of chalcedony and gold-veined quartz, of onyx and sardonyx, of porphyry and jasper, upheld fretted arches of a fashion lovelier than the arches of the Mosque of Cordova There were colonnades upon colonnades, domes rising above courts where silver fountains sang the songs of the Water-Spirit; here were minarets whose gilded crescents kissed the azure heaven; there were eunuchs, officers, executioners, viziers, odalisques, women graceful of form as undulating flame.

In a neighboring kingdom dwelt a sultry-eyed Sultana,—a daughter of sunrise, shaped of fire and snow, impulsive, generous, and far more potent than the Sultan. Either desired to become the friend of the other, but either feared to cross the line of purple hills which separated the kingdom. But they held communication by messengers. The Sultana's messengers always spoke the truth, yet scarcely spoke plainly, having great faith in diplomatic suggestion rather than in blunt and forcible utterance. The Sultan's messengers, on the other hand, only spoke half of the truth, being fearful lest their words should be overheard by the keen ears of men who desired that no courtesies should be exchanged between their mistress and her neighboring brother. At last the Sultana became wroth with a great wrath at the messengers, forasmuch as they conversed only in enigmas, the Sultana being apparently quite unable to imagine why they should so speak. Therefore the Sultana bound the messengers, stripped them naked, and, placing them in bags, despatched them by a camel caravan to the Sultan, expressing much anger at the conduct of the messengers. The Sultan, being alarmed at the detention of his messengers, knowing their proverbial loquacity, and fearing they had turned traitors, thanked Allah for their return, and swore by the Beard of his Father that ere sunrise they should die the death of cravens, inasmuch as they had not fulfilled their duty satisfactorily. He decided that they should be burnt with fire, and their ashes cast into the waters of the great river—

"sweeping down
Past carven pillars, under tamarisk groves
To where the broad sea sparkled."

"Kara-Mustapha," exclaimed the Sultan to his trusty vizier, "I desire the death of these dogs. May their fathers' graves be everlastingly defiled! Let them be burnt even as we burn the bones of the unclean beast. Let them be consumed in the furnaces of thy kitchen, that my viands may partake of a sweeter flavor." And so they died.

Meanwhile the Sultana repented of her wrath against the messengers, and despatched a sable eunuch in all haste to save them. But the eunuch arrived before midday, while the prince was yet in his harem dreaming of satiny-skinned houris and the flowers of the valley of Nourjahad, the fruits of the golden-leaved vines of Paradise, and the honeyed lips of the daughters of the prophet, which make mad those who kiss them with the madness of furious love. And the prince, being aroused by his favorite odalisque, lifted up his eyes and beheld the eunuch there standing with a message from the Sultana. And reading the message he fell from the tapestried couch upon the floor, exclaiming, "May all the Ghouls devour my father's bones, and may they tear and devour me when next I visit my mother's grave! By the beard of Allah, those messengers are not; they have died the dog's death, and have vanished even as the smoke of a narghile vanisheth." And a soft wind from the sensuous rosy-skied South toyed and caressed the volatile dust of the bones of the messengers; the dust fructified flowers of intoxicating perfume, and the spirit of the messengers melted into the glory of Paradise. There is but one God—Mahomet is his prophet. [*This is signed by a crescent and with L and H interwoven.*]

XII

DEAR LADY: I felt glad for divers reasons on receiving your letter and the little parcel,—firstly, because I felt that you were not very angry at my foolish fable; and secondly, because I always feel happy on having something nice to read. I had already read considerable of Darwin's "Voyages;" but just now I happened to desire a work of just that kind in order to educate myself in regard to certain ethnological points. I accept Darwin fully.

I do not believe in God—neither god of Greece nor of Rome nor any other god. I do indeed revere Woman as the creator, and I respect—yes, I almost believe in—the graceful Hellenic anthropomorphism which worshipped feminine softness and serpentine fascination and intoxicating loveliness in the garb of Venus Anadyomene. Yes, I could almost worship Aphrodite arisen, were there another renaissance of the antique paganism; and I feel all through me the spirit of that exquisite idolatry expressed in Swinburne's ode to "Our Lady of Pain." But I do not believe in Christ or in Christianity,—the former is not a grand character in my eyes, even as a myth; the latter I abhor as antagonistic to art, to nature, to passion, and to justice. As Théophile Gautier wrote, "I have never gathered passionflowers on the rocks of Calvary; and the river which flows from the flank of the Cross, making a crimson girdle about the world, has never bathed me with its waves."

I always take good care of books, and will return these you have so kindly lent me in a week or two.

Dear Lady, I am very anxious to be able to write that I have a week's freedom or a fortnight's holiday; and I promise you to let you know as soon as possible. But as yet I cannot leave my dull office,—the convention keeps us awfully busy. I would see you very often were it possible; but I never have more than a few hours' leisure daily.

XIII

I have still your letter,—I fancied it might be asked for again, but I do not like to return it, dear Lady,—I had rather make a Gheber sacrifice, and immolate Eros, a smiling and willing victim, to the White Lord of Fire.

No, I did not think the Sultana wicked; for I hold naught in human action to be evil save that which brings sorrow or pain to others. But even suppose the Sultana wicked for the sake of argument: her pretty and yet needless apology for the supposed mischief done was so tender, delicate, and uniquely fantastic that it would have earned the pardons supplicated for by ten thousand such peccadilloes. I could not forget it any more than I could forget the curves about the carved lips of the sweet Medicean Venus; it was a psychical blush of which the peculiar ruddiness made one long to see its twin.

This morning I found within my room a perfumed parcel, daintily odorous, containing diverse wonderful things, including a crystal vessel of remarkably peculiar design, very beautiful and very foreign. I thought of filling it with black volcanic wines, choleric and angry wine, in order to stimulate my resolution to the point of chiding the sender right severely. But the style of the vessel forbade; it was ruddily clear in the stained design, and icily brilliant elsewhere; it suggested the cold purity of a northern land,—fresh sea-breezes, fair hair, coolness of physical temperature. I concluded that nothing stronger than good brown ale would look at home therein; and this beverage provoketh good-nature.

I don't know how to reproach the author of this present properly. I shall not attempt it now. But I will certainly beg and entreat that I may not be favored with any more such kindnesses. I don't merit them, and feel the reverse of pleasant by accepting them. Why I don't know, but I never like to get presents some way or other. It is remarkably odd and pretty; so was the letter which accompanied it.

XIV

DEAR LADY: Notwithstanding your threat to leave my letters unopened, I will venture to write you a few lines. I think that you have misjudged me; and while fancying that I was treating you unkindly, you actually treated me somewhat unfairly,—without, of course, intending it. You have acted throughout, or nearly so, upon sudden impulse, which was injudicious; and when you found me acting in the opposite extreme, the necessary lack of sympathy in our actions prompted you to believe that I was "heartless." Now I can fully sympathize with your impulsiveness because I have had similar impulses; but I have been forced to control such impulses by the caution learned of unpleasant experiences. I will run no risks that could involve you or me,—especially you. I did not for one instant (and you only asserted the contrary through a spirit of mischievous reproach) think that I could not trust you with my letters. But I could not trust the letters....

I did not accept your last invitation only because I could not: it was of all weeks the busiest. I did not visit your home yesterday, because I had an assignment at the same hour in the east end, for the purpose of examining a smoke-consumer. If you had written me the day before, I could have made proper arrangements to come. You must think me capable of a little meanness to suppose that I would be discourteous enough to desire a *revanche* for your impulsive expression of an impulse. I understand why you returned my letter, and I could not feel offended.

XV

DEAR LADY: You must not ask me to forgive you, because I have nothing to forgive; and you must not speak of my being angry with you, because I was not angry with you at all. I wrote sharply, and perhaps disagreeably, because I felt that to do so would most speedily relieve you from your embarrassment; and sympathized sufficiently with your error to suffer with you. I entered into your feelings much more thoroughly, I believe, than you had any idea of, and I only deferred writing last night because I was fairly tired out with hard work. I have made many mistakes similar to yours; and felt similar regrets; and felt my face burn as though pricked with ten thousand needles, even when lying in bed in the dark, to think that a friend had betrayed some tender little confidence which might be turned into sinister ridicule. I was very, very sorry to feel that you had suffered similarly.

So, dear Lady, I feel generally very reluctant to unbosom myself on paper, not knowing who might behold the exposition, and sneer at it without being capable of understanding it. We all have two natures,—the one is our every-day garb of mannerism; the other we strived to keep draped, like a snow-limbed statue of Psyche, half guarded from unæsthetic eyes by a semi-diaphanous veil. This veiled nature is delicate as the wings of a butterfly, the gossamer web visible only when the sunlight catches it, or the frost-flowers on a window-pane. It will bear no rude touches—no careless handling. It is tenderer than the mythic blossom which bled when plucked, and its very tenderness enhances its capacity for suffering.

You may hear many things which on the impulse of the moment might affect you unpleasantly; but you need never yield to such an impulse. I am very well known in the city; and you might often hear people speak of me, but you must not think foolish things, or dream annoying dreams therefor....

What a funny little bundle of pretty contradictions your letter is! How can I answer it? By word of pen? No, not at all. I must only say that I like you quite as much—well, at least nearly as much—as you say that you wish. I won't say "quite," because I don't know myself, and how can I yet know you?

IONIKOE

XVI

DEAR LADY,—I remember having once been severely chided by a hoary friend of mine—a white-bearded Mentor—because I had just received a present from a friend, and had impulsively exclaimed, "Do tell me what I shall give him in return!" "Give in return!" quoth Mentor. "What for?—to destroy your little obligations of gratitude?—to insult your friend by practically intimating that you believe he expected something in return? Don't send him anything save thanks." Well, I didn't. But when I received your exquisite little gift this morning, I thought of writing, "How can I return your kindness," &c.; and now, calling my old friend's advice to mind, I shall only say, "Thanks, dear Lady." Still, flowers and me [sic] have so little in common, that much as I love them, I feel I ought not to be near them,— just as one who loves a woman so passionately that his dearest wish is to kiss her footprints; or as Kingsley's Norseman, who threw himself at the feet of the fair-haired priestess, crying, "Trample on me! spit on me! I am not worthy to be trod upon by your feet." Of course this is an extravagant simile; but the nature of a man is so coarse and rude compared with the fragrance and beauty of the flowers, that he feels in a purer atmosphere when they are breathing perfume about him. Flowers do seem to me like ghosts of maidens, like "that maid whom Gwydion made by glamour out of flowers."

Just fancy!—I was smoking a very poor cigar when the basket of blossoms came up to my rooms; and the odor of tobacco in the presence of the flowers seemed sacrilegious. I felt like the toad in Edgar Fawcett's poem. Perhaps you do not know that little poem, as it has not yet been published in book form. So I will quote it; but do not think me sentimental.

"TO A TOAD

"*Blue dusk, that brings the dewy hours,*
Brings thee, of graceless form in sooth,
Dark stumbler at the roots of flowers;
Flaccidy inert, uncouth.

- 62 -

"Right ill can human wonder guess
'Thy meaning or thy mission here,
Gray lump of mottled clamminess—
With that preposterous leer!

"But when I see thy dull bulk where
Luxurious roses bend and burny
Or some slim lily lifts to air
Her frail and fragrant urn,—

"Of these, among the garden ways,
So grim a watcher dost thou seem
That I, with meditative gaze
Look down on thee and dream

"Of thick-lipped slaves, with ebon skin,
That squat in hideous dumb repose
And guard the drowsy ladies in
Their still seraglios"

And talking of little roses, luxurious roses, I like them because of the fancies they evoke; their leaves and odor seem of kinship to the lips and the breath of a fair woman,—the lips of a woman humid with fresh kisses as the heart of the rose is humid with dews,—lips curled like the petals of the pink flower, recalling those of Swinburne's "Faustine"—

"Curled lips, long since half kissed away,
Still sweet and keen"

Dear lady, you sent me a very æsthetic present; and I fear I have written you a very sentimental letter. But if you don't want such effusions, you must not send me such flowers. I received your last few lines, and feel much relieved to find I have not offended you by my foolish letter. I cannot sit down late at night without saying something outrageous; and I must be possessed by the Devil of Heterophemy.

Very sincerely yours,

L. HEARN

Letters of Ozias Midwinter

"After this perhaps you will recognize the signature OZIAS MIDWINTER. It was taken from Wilkie Collins's 'Armadale.'" This brief postal-card message to his friend, Mr. Henry Watkin, written from New Orleans, November 15, 1877, is the valuable clue that leads to a discovery of a vein of work done by Lafcadio Hearn,—work that perhaps in after years he came to scorn, if not to forget. But for this information, imparted to a friend by Hearn himself, the "Letters of Ozias Midwinter" would doubtless lie undisturbed in their dusty tomb,—the files of the newspaper of yester-year. There may be those who will decry this resurrection of forgotten things; who will say it was the hack-work of a starving man; that it were better left undisturbed. They have a right to their opinion. Nevertheless, with due respect: to them, there are things in these letters as good as anything Hearn ever wrote. More than that, they reveal the whole trend of his mind; they foreshadow the things that were to interest him in the West Indies and in Japan,—the little mysteries of life, the poetry of names, the melody of folk-songs, the fascination of old things. The very adoption of the name of Ozias Midwinter is significant. Already at twenty-seven Hearn was too true a critic of real literature to imagine for a moment that "Armadale" was a book that was worth while; but there were things in this practically forgotten story that appealed to him with peculiar force, things that to him seemed almost as if they might have been written concerning himself. Hearn at times felt that his very name was ugly. In "Armadale" we read, "the strangely uncouth name of Ozias Midwinter;" and again: "It is so remarkably ugly that it must be genuine. No sane human being would, assume such a name as Ozias Midwinter."

His diminutive appearance was a sore point with Hearn. "Armadale" depicts Midwinter as "young and slim and under-sized."

There was something foreign-looking about Hearn. His fictional hero was thus described: "His tawny complexion, his large bright brown eyes, and his black beard gave him something of a foreign look.... His dusky hands were wiry and nervous."

Hearn, by reason of the peculiar appearance of his eyes, more often repelled than attracted people. He could therefore sympathize with Midwinter, who says:"I produced a disagreeable impression at first sight. I couldn't mend it afterwards."

A few more quotations will complete the picture and further make clear the fascination this character in a poor novel had for Hearn. The latter was from the start remarkably shy. He avoided the generality of men. For years he had been a failure in life. Everything he had tried had somehow fallen far below his expectations. Indeed, at the very time he was writing the Midwinter letters he was tramping the streets, going from newspaper office to office in New Orleans seeking work. Let us see now how these things in the life of Hearn correspond with the description of Midwinter: "From first to last the man's real character shrank back with a savage shyness from the rector's touch."

And again: "It mattered little what he tried: failure (for which nobody was ever to blame but himself) was sure to be the end of it, sooner or later. Friends to assist him he had none to apply to; and as for relations, he wished to be excused from speaking of them. For all he knew of them they might be dead, and for all they knew he might be dead."

And finally: "Ozias Midwinter at twenty spoke of his life as Ozias Midwinter at seventy might have spoken, with a long weariness of years on him which he had learned to bear patiently."

So much for the pseudonym. Now for the work to which it was attached. In after years, when Hearn had begun to attain a degree of prosperity, he either forgot something of the hard days, or, for some reason known to himself, told a pleasing fiction about them. Thus, in one letter that was made public shortly after his death, he says he went South from Cincinnati on a vacation, saw the blue and gold of Southern days, and determined to abide in such a climate forever. It has already been made clear in his letters to Mr. Watkin that he went South because the *wanderlust* was upon him, because he had begun to hate Cincinnati, because he felt that he must find more congenial work elsewhere. Whatever enthusiasts in Cincinnati and New Orleans may say now, he was not a good reporter in the present-day acceptance of the term. There was, on his part, a fancy for fine writing, for rhetoric, which the city editors of three decades ago may have admired, but which at present would be most vigorously blue-pencilled. A youthful Hearn to-day would have a rather hard time in Cincinnati, where the cry is for facts and again facts, and then for brevity and then once more for brevity. If Hearn did not come up to the modern standards of newspaper reporting, neither did he come up to the modern ideals of newspaper correspondence. It is probable that few papers to-day would tolerate the particular kind of "news letter" that Hearn sent to the Cincinnati *Commercial* in the years 1877 and 1878. It was in a day when the telegraph service was not so well developed as at present, and the news letters from Washington, Boston, New York, New Orleans, and London were a regular feature. There are few newspapers to-day which contain letters by men so eminent in after years as two of the *Commercial* correspondents became,—Hearn and

Moncure D. Conway, also for some time a resident of Cincinnati and afterwards correspondent from London.

Few if any of Hearn's "news letters" made any pretence at giving news. As far as the style of them was concerned, they might have been written for his friend Watkin alone, instead of for a great Ohio valley newspaper, catering to a considerable clientèle. He chose what subjects interested him, not what were presumed to interest the readers of the paper. In days when Louisiana's political affairs were still in the turmoil of the reconstruction period, when the North was still keenly watching events in the "rebel" South, Hearn had few if any references to these matters.

As near an approach as any to a news letter was his first one, sent from Memphis, November 6, 1877, when he wrote some "Notes on Forrest's Funeral." In this he related how he saw the funeral of General N. B. Forrest, the great Confederate cavalryman, told some anecdotes of the dead man's bravery and savagery, and gave his ancestry and an outline of his life.

Then he proceeded: "Old citizens of Memphis mildly described him to me as a 'terror.' He would knock a man down upon the least provocation, and whether with or without weapons, there were few people in the city whom he could not worst in a fight. Imagine a man about six feet three inches in height, very sinewy and active, with a vigorous, rugged face, bright grey eyes that almost always look fierce, eyebrows that seem always on the verge of a frown, and dark brown hair and chin beard, with strong inclination to curl, and you have some idea of Forrest's appearance before his last illness. He was, further, one of the most arbitrary, imperious, and determined men that it is possible to conceive of holding a high position in a civilized community. Rough, rugged, desperate, uncultured, his character fitted him rather for the life of the borderer than the planter; he seemed by nature a typical pioneer,—one of those fierce and terrible men who form in themselves a kind of protecting fringe to the borders of white civilization."

This is straightforward and vivid enough. But it was impossible for this dreamer of weird dreams to go through a whole letter in this fashion, and so we have the following, which, well written as it is, would scandalize the modern telegraph editor handling the correspondence: "The same night they buried him, there came a storm. From the same room whence I had watched the funeral, I saw the Northern mists crossing the Mississippi into Arkansas like an invading army; then came grey rain, and at last a fierce wind, making wild charges through it all. Somehow or other the queer fancy came to me that the dead Confederate cavalrymen, rejoined by their desperate leader, were fighting ghostly battles with the men who died for the Union."

The hustling, bustling Memphis of to-day is a far different place from the decayed, war-stricken town that the vagrant newspaper man saw. Its ruin, its damp days and nights, depressed him. In a letter of November 23, 1877, he recorded his impressions in a way that would doubtless to-day appeal strongly to the memory of the older generation of Memphians, who have not become used to the new order of things:

"The antiquity of the name of Memphis—a name suggesting vastness and ruin—compels something of a reverential feeling; and I approached the Memphis of the Mississippi dreaming solemnly of the Memphis of the Nile. I found the great cotton mart truly Egyptian in its melancholy decay, and not, therefore, wholly unworthy of its appellation. Tenantless warehouses with shattered windows; poverty-stricken hotels that vainly strive to keep up appearances; rows of once splendid buildings, from whose façades the paint has almost all scaled off; mock stone fronts, whence the stucco has fallen in patches, exposing the humble brick reality underneath; dinginess, dirt, and dismal dilapidation greet the eye at every turn. The city's life seems to have contracted about its heart, leaving the greater portion of its body paralyzed. Its commercial pulse appears to beat very feebly. It gives one the impression of a place that had been stricken by some great misfortune beyond hope of recovery. Yet Memphis still handles one fifth of the annual cotton crop,—often more than a million bales in a season,—and in this great branch of commerce the city will always hold its own, though fine buildings crumble and debts accumulate and warehouses lie vacant.... But when rain and white fogs come, the melancholy of Memphis becomes absolutely Stygian: all things wooden utter strange groans and crackling sounds; all things of stone or of stucco sweat as in the agony of dissolution, and beyond the cloudy brow of the bluffs the Mississippi flows dimly,—a spectral river, a Styx-flood, with pale mists lingering like Shades upon its banks, waiting for that ghostly ferryman, the wind."

In this letter occurred a quaint passage, illustrating at the same time the wide range of Hearn's reading and the curious paths into which he had allowed his mind to stray: "Elagabalus, wishing to obtain some idea of the vastness of imperial Rome, ordered all the cobwebs in the city to be collected together and heaped up before him. Estimated by such a method, the size of Memphis would appear vast enough to have astonished even Elagabalus."

However, brief as was his stay in Memphis, disagreeable as were most of his impressions, he found time to fall in love with one little piece of sculpture, thus charmingly described as "a little nude Venus at the street fountain, who has become all of one dusky greyish-green hue, preserving her youth only in the beauty of her rounded figure and unwrinkled comeliness of face." In this letter he detailed something of his journey down the river, chronicled his delight in the Southern sunsets, and finally arrived at the first of his promised lands: "The daylight faded away, and the stars came out, but that warm glow in the southern horizon only paled so that it seemed a little further off. The river broadened till it looked, with the tropical verdure of its banks, like the Ganges, until at last there loomed up a vast line of shadows, dotted with points of light, and through a forest of masts and a host of phantom-white river boats and a wilderness of chimneys the *Thompson Dean*, singing her cheery challenge, steamed up to the mighty levee of New Orleans."

In his next letter, dated November 26, 1877, he described his first impressions "at the gates of the Tropics." He came across things that reminded him of London and of Paris and evoked memories of his youth:

"Eighteen miles of levee! London, with all the gloomy vastness of her docks and her 'river of ten thousand masts,' can offer no spectacle so picturesquely attractive and so varied in the attraction." And again: "Canal Street, with its grand breadth and imposing façades, gives one recollections of London and Oxford Street and Regent Street." He went to the French market, still one of the great sights of the city, and could not write enough about it:

"The markets of London are less brightly clean and neatly arranged; the markets of Paris are less picturesque." Even a cotton-press seen at the cotton landing was an event to be celebrated. The thing was to him not merely a piece of ingenious machinery; it was something weird, something demoniac: "Fancy a monstrous head of living iron and brass, fifty feet high from its junction with the ground, having jointed gaps in its face like Gothic eyes, a mouth five feet wide, opening six feet from the mastodon teeth in the lower jaw to the mastodon teeth in the upper jaw. The lower jaw alone moves, as in living beings, and it is worked by two vast iron tendons, long and thick and solid as church pillars. The surface of this lower jaw is equivalent to six square feet. The more I looked at the thing, the more I felt as though its prodigious anatomy had been studied after the anatomy of some extinct animal,—the way those jaws worked, the manner in which those muscles moved. Men rolled a cotton bale to the mouth of the monster. The jaws opened with a low roar, and so remained. The lower jaw had descended to the level with the platform on which the bale was lying. It was an immense plantation bale. Two black men rolled it into the yawning mouth. The titan muscles contracted, and the jaws closed, silently, steadily, swiftly. The bale flattened, flattened, flattened down to sixteen inches, twelve inches, eight inches, five inches,—positively less than five inches! I thought it was going to disappear altogether. But after crushing it beyond five inches the jaw remained stationary and the monster growled like rumbling thunder. I thought the machine began to look as hideous as one of those horrible yawning heads which formed the gates of the teocallis at Palenque, and through whose awful jaws the sacrificial victims passed."

On December 7, 1877, he dived into more serious and even more practical things. This man, to whom colored races were always of the deepest interest, who had prowled around the negro quarters of Cincinnati for songs and melodies and superstitions, around the Chinese laundries for chance discoveries of strange musical instruments from the Orient, after a residence in the South of one month, discussed a question which is still agitating the country and which threatens to trouble it for many years to come,—the negro question. Charles Gayarré of Louisiana had written an article for the *North American Review* entitled "The Southern Question." Hearn, who certainly cannot be accused of prejudice against colored peoples, agreed with the Southern writer that white supremacy was necessary for Southern peace and prosperity. He felt that the particular menace of the whites was from the mixed breeds, whose black blood had just enough alloy to make them despise the simplicity and faithfulness of the lowly "darky" of the old régime and aspire to more rights and more privileges. Recently a Southern thinker has written a book to show that, in the inexorable law of the survival of the fittest, the ten million negroes must be swept aside by the seventy million whites of this land, and finally perish from the face of the earth, as do all the weaker races. Nearly three decades ago Hearn came to the same conclusion,—a conclusion not expressed without some feeling of fondness for the race: "As for the black man, he must disappear with the years. Dependent like the ivy, he needs some strong oak-like friend to cling to. His support has been cut from him, and his life must wither in its prostrate helplessness. Will he leave no trace of his past in the fields made fertile by his mighty labors, no memory of his presence in this fair land he made rich in vain? Ah, yes! the echo of the sweetly melancholy songs of slavery,—the weird and beautiful melodies born in the hearts of the poor, childlike people to whom freedom was destruction."

By the time he sent his next letter, dated December 10, 1877, he had again been wandering about the city. He visited the old Spanish cathedral founded by Don Andre Almonaster, Regidor and Alferez Real of his Most Catholic Majesty. This is the church that is always referred to as the "French cathedral." Hearn described its two ancient tombs,—that of Almonaster, who died in 1708, and then that of the French noble family of De Marigny de Mandeville, scions of which died and were buried there in 1728, 1779, and 1800. Hearn had his own reflections over the matter just as Irving had in Westminster Abbey:

"O Knights of the Ancient Régime, the feet of the plebeians are blotting out your escutcheons; the overthrowers of throned Powers pass by your tombs with a smile of complacency; the callous knees of the poorest poor will erelong obliterate your carven memory from the stone; the very places of your dwelling have crumbled out of sight and out of remembrance. The glory of Versailles has passed away; 'the spider taketh hold with his hands, and is in the palaces of Kings.'"

From musings in the cathedral he passed into a disquisition on language. He held that the French tongue sounded better to him from the mouth of a negro than did the harsher English. Southern speech flows melodiously from the negro's lips, being musically akin to the many-vowelled languages of Africa. The *th's* and *thr's*, the difficult diphthongs and guttural *rr's* of English and German, have a certain rude Northern strength beyond the mastery of Ethiopian lips. He finds that the Louisiana blacks speak a corrupted French, often called "Creole," which is not the Creole of the Antilles. This recalls to him a memory of his childhood in England and gives also a foretaste of what he was to do ten years later, when Harpers gave him a chance to describe what he felt and saw in the French West Indies:

"Yesterday evening, the first time for ten years, I heard again that sweetest of all dialects, the Creole of the Antilles. I had first heard it spoken in England by the children of an English family from Trinidad, who were visiting relatives in the mother country, and I could never forget its melody. In Martinique and elsewhere it has almost a written dialect; the school-children used to study the 'Creole catechism,' and priests used to preach to their congregations in Creole. You cannot help falling in love with it after having once heard it spoken by young lips, unless indeed you have no poetry in your composition, no music in your soul. It is the most liquid, mellow, languid language in the world. It is especially a language for love-making. It sounds like pretty baby-talk; it woos like the cooing of a dove. It seems to be a mixture of French, a little Spanish, and West African dialects,—those negro dialects that are voluminous with vowels. You can imagine how smooth it is from the fact that in West Indian Creole the letter *r* is never pronounced; and the Europeans of the Indies complain that once their children have learned to speak Creole, it is hard to teach them to pronounce any other language correctly. They will say 'b'ed' for bread and 't'ed' for thread. So that it is a sort of wopsy-popsy-ootsy-tootsy language."

And from this affectionate passage he is led to speak of Creole satires. During the Republican régime in New Orleans after the Civil War there was a witty, bitter, and brilliant French paper called *Le Carillon*, which designated Republicans by a new term, "Radicanailles," which seemed exceedingly satisfying to the proud aristocracy,—this word compounded of "radical" and *"canaille"* The paper used to print Creole satires. One was on ex-Governor Antoine, in the form of a parody upon "La Fille de Madame

Angot." Now Hearn's ambition was to write a sinuous, silvern, poetical prose. He rarely attempted verse. In his better known books on Japan his versions of Japanese songs and poems are in prose. So, too, in these letters all his renderings of the things that attracted him are in prose. Here is his version of the satire just mentioned, redolent as it is of an era of bitterness:

I

"In the old days before the war, I was a slave at Caddo [Parish]. I tilled the earth and raised sweet potatoes and water-melons. Then afterwards I left the plough and took up the razor to shave folks in the street,—white and black, too. But that, that was before the war.

II

"When Banks went up the river (Red River) with soldiers and with cannon, I changed my career. Then I became a runaway slave. I married my own cousin, who is at this hour my wife. She—she attended to the kitchen. I—I sought for honors. But that, that was during the war.

III

"And then afterward in the custom-house men called me Collector; and then Louisiana named me her Senator; and then to show her confidence the people made me Governor and called me His Eminence; and that is what I am at this present hour. And that, that is since the war."

From this, with the inconsequential air of a butterfly, he turned to the subject of the Greeks of New Orleans,—a subject that must have lain near to his heart by reason of the deep love he bore for his Greek mother. Among the New Orleans people he mentioned was one Greek gentleman: "I never met a finer old man. Though more than seventy years of age, his face was still as firmly outlined, as clearly cut, as an antique cameo; its traits recalled memories of old marbles, portraits in stone of Aristophanes and Sophocles; it bespoke a grand blending of cynicism and poetry."

But the sons of Hellas were not all alike satisfactory to his fastidious taste: "There are many Greeks, sailors and laborers, in New Orleans; but I cannot say that they inspire one with dreams of Athens or of Corinth, of Panathenaic processions or Panhellenic games. Their faces are not numismatic; their forms are not athletic. Sometimes you can discern a something national about a Greek steamboatman,—a something characteristic which distinguishes him from the equally swarthy Italian, Spaniard, 'Dago.' But that something is not of antiquity; it is not inspirational. It is Byzantine, and one is apt to dislike it. It reminds one of Taine's merciless criticism of the faces of Byzantine art. But I have seen a few rare Hellenic types here, and among these some beautiful Romaic girls,—maidens with faces to remind you of the gracious vase paintings of antiquity." One would think he had crammed this letter full enough of topics, but he had one more. Throughout his life ghost stories were an obsession with him. They run all through his books on Japan. Three decades ago he lamented: "In these days ghosts have almost lost the power to interest us, for we have become too familiar with their cloudy faces, and familiarity begetteth contempt. An original ghost story is a luxury, and a rare luxury at that."

He then told of a house on Melpomene Street, New Orleans, in which no one could dwell in peace. If a person were so hardy and so skeptical as to move in, he soon found his furniture scattered, and his carpets torn up by invisible hands. Ghostly feet shook the house with their terrible steps; ghostly hands opened bolted doors as if locks did not exist,—so that by and by no one came to live in the old place any more:

"As the years flitted by the goblin of Decay added himself to the number of the Haunters; the walls crumbled, and the floors yielded, and grass, livid and ghastly looking grass, forced its pale way between the chinks of the planks in the parlor. The windows fell into ruin, and the wind entered freely to play with the ghosts, and cried weirdly in the vacant room.'

Then one night Chief of Police Leary and six of his most stalwart men determined to stand watch in the building and solve the mystery. They placed candles in one of the rooms, and towards midnight stood in a hollow square, with Chief Leary in the middle, so that he could aid his men to repel an attack from any quarter whatsoever. The ghosts blew out the lighted candles and, to this extent, were commonplace enough. But the next instant they displayed their complete ingenuity and originality by seizing the seven guardians of the peace and hurling them violently against the ceiling. Hearn adds, with a touch of playful humor: "The city of New Orleans would not pay the doctors' bills of men injured while in the discharge of their duty."

By December 17, 1877, he had become interested in the past and present of "Los Criollos," the Creoles, who were to be such a fascinating subject to him when he visited Martinique and other enchanted isles of the Caribbean.

In this first letter on the subject he corrected the common error of speaking of mulattoes, quadroons, and octaroons of Louisiana as Creoles,—a mistake which curiously enough he himself made in his book, "Ghombo Zhebes," several years later. In this letter, however, he correctly pointed out that no person with the slightest taint of negro blood was a Creole, and that the common mistake was made not only in the North, but also often in the South, where they should know better; not only in America, but also in England, France, and Spain, the former mother countries of all the West Indian colonists. "Creole," properly speaking, is the term applied to the pure-blooded offspring of Europeans born in the colonies of South America or the West Indies, to distinguish them from children of mixed blood born in the colonies or of pure blood born in the mother country. In Louisiana, he pointed out that it usually meant they were of French, more rarely of Spanish, descent. He paid a tribute to the Creole society of New Orleans which was made up of the descendants of all the early European settlers: "Something of all that was noble and true and brilliant in the almost forgotten life of the dead South lives here still (its atmosphere is European; its tastes are governed by European literature and the art culture of the Old World)." Hethen quoted some of the poems in the patois of Louisiana and also some from Martinique that he had already picked up.

On December 22 he devoted his attention to "New Orleans in Wet Weather." He had much to say of its dampness and chills and fogs: "Strange it is to observe the approach of one of these eerie fogs on some fair night. The blue deeps above glow tenderly beyond the sharp crescent of the moon; the heavens seem transformed to an infinite ocean of liquid turquoise, made living with the palpitating life of the throbbing stars. In this limpid clearness, this yellow, tropical moonlight, objects are plainly visible at a distance of miles; far sounds come to the ear with marvellous distinctness,—the clarion calls of the boats, the long, loud panting of the cotton-presses, exhaling steaming breath from their tireless lungs of steel.

"Suddenly sounds become fainter and fainter, as though the atmosphere were made feeble by unaccountable enchantment; distant objects lose distinctness; the heaven is cloudless, but her lights, low-burning and dim, no longer make the night transparent, and a chill falls upon the city, such as augurs the coming of a ghost. Then the ghost appears; the invisible makes itself visible; a vast form of thin white mist seems to clasp the whole night in its deathly embrace; the face of the moon is hidden as with a grey veil, and the spectral fog extinguishes with its chill breath the trembling flames of the stars."

Turning his thought to grave matters, he refers to the elevated tombs in the cemeteries, which some irreverently call "bake ovens." Then comes a touch of the playful, familiar enough to those who read the present volume, but rare in his other books: "Fancy being asked by a sexton whether you wished to have the remains of your wife or child deposited in 'one of them bake ovens.'"

Again, with a swift turn of thought and subject, as if in conversation with a friend or as if in a letter to him, he reverts to "Beast Ben Butler" and his needless brutality in having carved on one of the New Orleans statues,

Clay's declaration against slavery and Andrew Jackson's famous saying, "Our federal Union: it must be preserved." The sight of Levantine sailors selling fruit in the markets caused him to rhapsodize on the sea, giving the first of those prose poems in which he was to wax almost lyrical in so many of his works: "If you, O reader, chance to be a child of the sea; if, in earliest childhood, you listened each morning and evening to that most ancient and mystic hymn-chant of the waves, which none can hear without awe, and which no musician can learn; if you have ever watched wonderingly the far sails of the fishing vessels turn rosy in the blush of the sunset, or silver under the moon, or golden in the glow of sunrise; if you once breathed as your native air the divine breath of the ocean, and learned the swimmer's art from the hoary breakers, and received the Ocean god's christening, the glorious baptism of salt,—then perhaps you know only too well why those sailors of the Levant cannot seek homes within the heart of the land. Twenty years may have passed since your ears last caught the thunder of that mighty ode of hexameters which the sea has always sung and will sing forever,—since your eyes sought the far line where the vaulted blue of heaven touches the level immensity of rolling waters,—since you breathed the breath of the ocean, and felt its clear ozone living in your veins like an elixir. Have you forgotten the mighty measure of that mighty song? Have you forgotten the divine saltiness of that unfettered wind? Is not the spell of the sea strong upon you still?...

"And I think that the Levantine sailors dare not dwell in the midst of the land, for fear lest dreams of a shadowy sea might come upon them in the night, and phantom winds call wildly to them in their sleep, and they might wake to find themselves a thousand miles beyond the voice of the breakers."

On December 27, 1877, already deeply interested in the niceties of language, Hearn gave his Cincinnati readers a dissertation upon the curiosities of Creole grammar, and quoted in Creole a weird love-song, said to be of negro origin. He doubted whether it was really composed by a negro, but remarked that its spirit was undoubtedly African. Then he gave the following prose version of this exotic:

"Since first I beheld you, Adele,
While dancing the calinda,
I have remained faithful to the thought of you;
My freedom has departed from me,
I care no longer for all other negresses;
I have no heart left for them;—
You have such grace and cunning:—
You are like the Congo serpent.

"I love you too much, my beautiful one:—
I am not able to help it.
My heart has become just like a grasshopper,—
It does nothing but leap.
I have never met any woman
Who has so beautiful a form as yours.
Your eyes flash flame;
Your body has enchained me captive.

"Ah, you are so like the serpent-of-the-rattles
Who knows how to charm the little bird,
And who has a mouth ever ready for it
Yo serve it for a tomb.
I have never known any negress
Who could walk with such grace as you can.
Or who could make such beautiful gestures;
Your body is a beautiful doll.

"When I cannot see you, Adele,
I feel myself ready to die;
My life becomes like a candle
Which has almost burned itself out.
I cannot then find anything in the world
Which is able to give me pleasure:—
I could well go down to the river
And throw myself in it that I might cease to suffer.

Tell me if you have a man,
And I will make an ouanga charm for him:
I will make him turn into a phantom,
If you will only take me for your husband.
I will not go to see you when you are cross;
Other women are mere trash to me;
I will make you very happy
And I will give you a beautiful Madras handkerchief."

He freely admitted that the poem was untranslatable, that it lost its weird beauty, its melody, its liquid softness, its languor, when put into English. Then came a characteristic bit in which he displayed the man who dwelt with delight upon the inner meaning of words,—the delight felt only by the artist in language: "I think there is some true poetry in these allusions to the snake. Is not the serpent a symbol of grace? Is not the so-called 'line of beauty' serpentine? And is there not something of the serpent in the beauty of all graceful women? something of undulating shapeliness, something of silent fascination? something of Lilith and Lamia? The French have a beautiful verb expressive of this idea,—*serpenter*, 'to serpent,' to curve in changing undulations like a lithe snake. The French artist speaks of the outlines of a beautiful human body as serpenting,' curving and winding like a serpent. Do you not like the word? I think it is so expressive of flowinglines of elegance,—so full of that mystery of grace which puzzled Solomon: 'the way of a serpent upon a rock.'"

On January 7, 1878, came a picture in prose, which now reminds us of William Ernest Henley's "London Voluntary," in which the latter described the splendor of a golden October day in the metropolis of the world. Here is Christmas Eve in New Orleans: "Christmas Eve came in with a blaze of orange glory in the west, and masses of lemon-colored clouds piled up above the sunset. The whole city was filled with orange-colored light, just before the sun went down; and between the lemon-hued clouds and the blue were faint tints of green. The colors of that sunset seemed a fairy mockery of the colors of the fruit booths throughout the city; where the golden fruit lay piled up in luxuriant heaps, and where the awnings of white canvas had been replaced by long archways of interwoven orange branches with the fruit still glowing upon them. It was an Orange Christmas."

Then at nightfall he passed the French opera house on Bourbon Street. It was "dark and dead and silent," and as a matter of course the dreamer had another vision: "Sometimes, when passing under the sharply cut shadows of the building in a night of tropical moonlight, I fancy that a shadowy performance of 'Don Giovanni' or 'Masaniello' must be going on within for the entertainment of a ghostly audience; and that if somebody would but open the doors an instant, one might catch a glimpse of spectral splendor, of dusky-eyed beauties long dead,—of forgotten faces pale with the sleep of battlefields,—of silks that should be mouldering in mouldering chests with the fashions of twenty years ago."

And finally this letter contained the following prophetic utterance concerning the new South,—the South then not yet in existence, the South that so nearly approximates what Hearn said it would be: "It is the picturesqueness of the South, the poetry, the traditions, the legends, the superstitions, the quaint faiths, the family prides, the luxuriousness, the splendid indolence and the splendid sins of the old social system which have passed, or which are now passing, away forever.... The new South may, perhaps, become far richer than the old South; but there will be no aristocracy, no lives of unbridled luxury, no reckless splendors of hospitality, no mad pursuit of costliest pleasures. The old hospitality has been starved to death, and leaves no trace of its former being save the thin ghost of a romance. The new South will be less magnificent, though wealthier; less generous, though more self-denying; less poetical, though more cultured. The new cities will be, probably, more prosperous and less picturesque than the old."

January 14, 1878, Hearn devoted his entire letter to W. C. C. Claiborne, the first American governor of Louisiana. He told in what hostile manner the American was received by the haughty Creole gentry, and how he was alleged to have worn his hat at the theatre. It is in the comment on this that Hearn most amusingly displays himself as an Englishman, with the dim-seeing eyes of a Dickens or a saucy Kipling rather than the clear-headed, clear-eyed American, or the adopted citizen, understanding this country and its people: "I fancy that wearing of the hat before those terribly cultivated and excruciatingly courteous Creole audiences must have been at first a mere oversight; but that poor Claiborne naturally got stubborn when such an outcry was raised about it and, with an angry pride of manhood peculiar to good American blood, swore 'by the Eternal' that he would wear his hat wherever he pleased. Don't you almost wish you could slap him on the shoulder with that truly American slap of approbation?" Of course that is pure Dickens, the Dickens of "American Notes," just as is the following rather amusing description of American newspapers in the good years 1804, 1805, and 1806: "In those days the newspaper seems to have been neither more nor less than a public spittoon,—every man flung his quid of private opinion into it."

Hearn went to look at the Claiborne graves in the old St. Louis cemetery on Basin Street. Throughout his life graveyards seemed to have a fascination for him; but the following description of the St. Louis cemetery is interesting because it proves, what has often been denied, that part of Hearn's boyhood was spent in Wales: "This cemetery is one of the most curious, and at the same time one of the most dilapidated, in the world. I have seen old graveyards in the north of England, and tombs in Wales, where names of the dead of three hundred years ago may yet be read upon the mossy stones; but I have never seen so grim a necropolis as the ruined Creole cemetery at New Orleans. There is no order there, no regularity, no long piles of white obelisks, no even ranks of grey tablets. The tombs seem to jostle one another; the graveyard is a labyrinth in which one may easily lose oneself. Some of the tombs are Roman in size and design; some are mere heaps of broken brick; some are of the old-fashioned table form."

Readers of Hearn's books are familiar with those pages in which he speaks of Japanese female names, and studies appellations in general. This fancy was no new thing with him. As long ago as February 18, 1878, he studied the curious nomenclature of New Orleans streets, revealing, as it does, part of the history of the city, something of its old gallant life, something of its old classical culture. He told how Burgundy Street was named after the great duke; Dauphine is, of course, self-explanatory, as are Louis XV and

Royal and Bourbon. Governors are represented by Carondelet, Galvez, and others; French and Spanish piety, by such names as St. Bartholomy, St. Charles, and Annunciata. The classicism, which so affected the traditions of French poetry and the French stage, is here represented by-streets named Calliope, Clio, Dryades, &c. Gallantry, "often wicked gallantry, I fear," is commemorated by a number of streets christened with "the sweetest and prettiest feminine names imaginable,—Adele, Celeste, Suzette, and Annette."

Then he gave his readers some more of those Creole songs he was always collecting, some of which as rich treasure he was afterwards to give to his friend, Mr. H. E. Krehbiel, the musical critic. In this letter he told how, when for the first time he read Daudet's novel, translated under the title of "Sidonie," he was charmed with the refrain of a Creole song, and determined, when in New Orleans, to procure the whole poem. He recorded his disappointment in being able only to get one stanza, which he translated as follows:

"Others say it is your happiness;
I say, it is your sorrow:
When we are enchanted by love,
Farewell to all happiness!
Poor little Miss Zizi!
Poor little Miss Zizi!
Poor little Miss Zizi!
She has sorrow, sorrow, sorrow;—
She has sorrow in her heart!"

Here is another bit, which seems to the Anglo-Saxon very uncouth and unpoetical when given in bare, bald English, robbed of the oft-lisping Creole melody:

"If thou wert a little bird,
And I were a little gun,
I would shoot thee—bang!
Ah, dear little
Mahogany jewel,
I love thee as a little pig loves the mud?'

The next is more charming. It is only a snatch, but it hints delicious romance:

"Delaide, my queen, the way is too long for me to travel;—
That way leads far up yonder.
But, little as I am, I am going to stem the stream up there.

'*I, Liron, am come,' is what I shall say to them.*
'*My queen, good night; 'tis I, Liron, who have come.'*"

And finally there is this one, evidently of negro origin, made to ridicule a mulatto girl named Toucouton, who tried to pass as white:

"*Ah, Toucouton!*
I know you well:
You are like a blackamoor;
There is no soap
Which is white enough
To wash your skin.

"*When the white folks give a ball,*
You are not able to go there;
Ah, how will you be able to play the flirt!
You who so love to shine?
Ah, Toucouton, &c.

"*Once you used to take a seat*
Among the fashionable people;
Now you must take leave, decamps
Without any delay whatever.
Ah, Toucouton," &c.

We have seen that all these letters by Hearn were as if written for his own pleasure or for the pleasure of a friend, but decidedly not for a newspaper clientèle. After the "news" just referred to, there followed two letters which would seem to indicate that the patient editor besought his correspondent to come nearer to hard, prosaic news matters and treat of the turmoil of Louisiana state affairs. Accordingly, on March 24, 1878, there was a screed on of "Louisiana as It Is," treating of the political questions, and finally another, on March 31, scouting the possibility of forming a Hayes party in Louisiana. These letters were written in so half-hearted a way that it was not at all surprising to see the next letter from New Orleans signed by a new and more ordinary name. Hearn was no longer the representative of the paper. He went on record to the effect that he quit because the paper was slow about paying him money, although he demanded the arrears time and time again. The chances are that the *Commercial's* readers stupidly wanted more about politics and less about Creole love poetry. With the close of this correspondence Hearn thus definitely closed all connexion with the Cincinnati newspaper world.

We have seen now, from the Midwinter letters, how the Hearn of New Orleans was the father of the Hearn of the West Indies and of Japan.

Indeed, so far as his work was concerned, the same subjects interested him throughout his life. This is not to say that he remained at a standstill. On the contrary, he was constantly growing. Despite his bad eyesight, he read incessantly, and his reading took a very wide range. He labored to perfect his style. He struggled with words; he used the file after a fashion to remind one of what Flaubert and Stevenson have told us of themselves. But with a very wise knowledge of his own sympathies and limitations, he chose exactly the topics for his pen that could most surely stir his imagination. It is a little singular, some seven years after his letters to the Cincinnati newspaper, to find him writing practically the same kind of articles and on the same subjects for *Harper's Weekly*. Hearn, then at the age of thirty-five, anxious to have his things appear in some publication with a circulation other than purely local, and anxious likewise to eke out his slender income, managed to secure a commission from the house of Harper. The firm had sent a staff artist to New Orleans to draw sketches of the exposition of 1885. Hearn was to supply the descriptive articles. His first appeared in *Harper's Weekly* of January 3, 1885, and was a straightforward account of the exposition. Of course with a man of Hearn's temperament this could not last long, so it is not surprising to see the next letter, which appeared on January 10, 1885, devoted to "The Creole Patois."

"Although," he writes, "the pure Creole element is disappearing from the 'Vie Faubon,' as Creole children call the antiquated part of New Orleans, it is there, nevertheless, that the patois survives as a current idiom; it is there one must dwell to hear it spoken in its purity and to study its peculiarities of intonation and construction. The patois-speaking inhabitants, dwelling mostly in those portions of the quadrilateral furthest from the river and from the broad American boundary of Canal Street,—which many of them never cross when they can help it,—are not less bizarre than the architectural background of their picturesque existence. The visitor is surrounded by a life motley-colored as those fantastic populations described in the Story of the Young King of the Black Isles; the African ebon is least visible, but of bronze browns, banana yellows, orange golds, there are endless varieties, paling off into faint lemon tints and even dead silver whites. The paler the shade, the more strongly do Latin characteristics show themselves; and the oval faces, with slender cheeks and low, broad brows, prevail. Sometimes in the yellower types a curious Sphinx visage appears, dreamy as Egypt. Occasionally also one may encounter figures so lithe, so animal, as to recall the savage grace of Piou's 'Satyress.' For the true colorist the contrast of a light saffron skin with dead black hair and eyes of liquid jet has a novel charm, as of those descriptions in the Malay poem, Bida-sari,' of 'women like statues of gold.' It is hard to persuade oneself that such types do not belong to one distinct race, the remnant of some ancient island tribe, and the sound of their richly vowelled Creole speech might prolong the pleasant illusion."

Happening to mention an ocoroon, the very term starts him on a rhapsody:

"That word reminds one of a celebrated and vanished type,—never mirrored upon canvas, yet not less physically worthy of artistic preservation than those amber-tinted beauties glorified in the Oriental studies of Ingres, of Richter, of Gérôme! Uncommonly tall were those famous beauties, citrine-hued, elegant of stature as palmettoes, lithe as serpents; never again will such types reappear upon American soil. Daughters of luxury, artificial human growths, never organized to enter the iron struggle for life unassisted and unprotected, they vanished forever with the social system which made them a place apart as for splendid plants reared within a conservatory. With the fall of American feudalism the dainty glass house was dashed to pieces; the species it contained have perished utterly; and whatever morality may have gained, one cannot help thinking that art has lost something by their extinction. What figures for designs in bronze! What tints for canvas!"

Then Hearn returns to the subject of the Creoles, and speaks of the compilation of Creole proverbs of the Antilles and other places, but of the lack of a similar work in Louisiana. It foreshadowed his own "Ghombo Zhebes," then in the making. Reading his description of the fugitive Creole literature, one regrets that Hearn did not find time and opportunity to collect: it as he did the proverbs.

"The inedited Creole literature," says he, "comprised songs, satires in rhyme, proverbs, fairy tales,—almost everything commonly included under the term of folk-lore. The lyrical portion of it is opulent in oddities, in melancholy beauties; Alphonse Daudet has frequently borrowed therefrom, using Creole refrains in his novels with admirable effect. Some of the popular songs possess a unique and almost weird pathos; there is a strange, naïve sorrow in their burdens, as of children sobbing for lonesomeness in the night. Others, on the contrary, are inimitably comical. There are many ditties or ballads devoted to episodes of old plantation life, to surreptitious frolic, to description of singular industries and callings, to commemoration of events which had strongly impressed the vivid imagination of negroes,— a circus show, an unexpected holiday, the visit of a beautiful stranger to the planter's home, or even some one of those incidents indelibly marked with a crimson spatter upon the fierce history of Louisiana politics."

On January 17, under the same caption, Hearn continued the subject, giving some of the songs and speaking of their probable African ancestry.

On January 31, once more under the general title of "The New Orleans Exposition," Hearn turns with avidity to musings on the Japanese exhibit. Right in the beginning we have this on art, remarkable, as so much of Hearn's work was, for a vivid sense of color and form despite his own difficulty in seeing: "What Japanese art of the best era is unrivalled in—that characteristic in which, according even to the confession of the best French art connoisseurs, it excels all other art—is movement, the rhythm, the poetry of visible motion. Great masters of the antique Japanese schools have been known to devote a whole lifetime to the depiction of one kind of bird, one variety of insect or reptile, alone. This specialization of art, as Ary Renan admirably showed us in a recent essay, produced results that no European master has ever been able to approach. A flight of gulls sweeping through the gold light of a summer morning; a long line of cranes sailing against a vermilion sky; a swallow twirling its kite shape against the disk of the sun; the heavy, eccentric, velvety flight of bats under the moon; the fairy hoverings of moths or splendid butterflies,—these are subjects the Japanese brush has rendered with a sublimity of realism which might be imitated, perhaps, but never surpassed. Except in the statues of gods or goddesses (Buddhas which almost compel the Christian to share the religious awe of their worshippers, or those charming virgins of the Japanese heaven, 'slenderly supple as a beautiful lily'), the Japanese have been far from successful in delineation of the human figure. But their sculpture or painting of animal forms amazes by its grace; their bronze tortoises, crabs, storks, frogs, are not mere copies of nature: they are exquisite idealizations of it."

Almost every paragraph seems to foreshadow some chapter in some one of Hearn's future books on Japan. With a memory of his papers on Japanese inserts, this, written in 1885, is significant:

"Perhaps it is bad taste on the writer's part, but the bugs and reptiles in cotton attracted his attention even more than the cranes. You see a Japanese tray covered with what appear to be dead and living bugs and beetles,—some apparently about to fly away; others with upturned abdomen, legs shrunk up, antennae inert. They are so life-like that you may actually weigh one in your hand a moment before you find that it is made of cotton. Everything, even to the joints of legs or abdomen, is exquisitely imitated: the metallic lustre of the beetle's armor is reproduced by a bronze varnish. There are cotton crickets with the lustre of lacquer, and cotton grasshoppers of many colors: the korogi, whose singing is like to the sound of a weaver, weaving rapidly ('ko-ro-ru, ko-ro-ru'), and the kirigisi, whose name is an imitation of its own note."

Or again, remembering his masterly description of an ascent of the famous Japanese mountain, read this, written long before he had ever seen it in the reality: "Splendid silks were hanging up everywhere, some exquisitely embroidered with attractive compositions, figures, landscapes, and especially views of Fusiyama, the matchless mountain, whose crater edges are shaped like the eight petals of the Sacred Lotos; Fusiyama, of which the great artist Houkousai alone drew one hundred different views; Fusiyama, whose snows may only be compared for pearly beauty to 'the white teeth of a young girl,' and whose summit magically changes its tints through the numberless variations of light. Everywhere it appears,—the wonderful mountain,—on fans, behind rains of gold, or athwart a furnace light of sunset, or against an immaculate blue, or gold burnished by some wizard dawn; in bronze, exhaling from its mimic crater a pillar of incense smoke; on porcelain, towering above stretches of vineyard and city-speckled plains, or perchance begirdled by a rich cloud sash of silky, shifting tints, like some beauty of Yosiwara."

At this period in his life there was not only a love of Creole folk-lore and a longing for Japan, but a very decided and deep interest in things Chinese. Not only was Hearn preparing himself for the writing of "Some Chinese Ghosts," but it is altogether probable that his dreams of a trip to Asia contemplated a sojourn in China as well as in Japan. The daintiness, the fairy-like beauty of the Island Empire won him, and China lost its chance for interpretation by a master. However, in his letter of March 7, 1885, telling of "The East at New Orleans," we find this relative to China:

"At either side of the main entrance is a great vase, carved from lips to base with complex designs in partial relief and enamelled in divers colors. In general effect of coloration the display is strictly Chinese; the dominating tone is yellow,—bright yellow, the sacred and cosmogonic color according to Chinese belief. When the Master of Heaven deigns to write, He writes with yellow ink only, save when He takes the lightning for His brush to trace a white sentence of destruction. So at least we are told in the book called Kan-ing p'ien,—the 'Book of Rewards and Punishments,' which further describes the writing of God as being in *tchouen*,—those antique 'seal-characters' now rarely seen except in jewel engraving, signatures stamped on works of art, or inscriptions upon monuments,—those primitive ideographic characters dating back perhaps to that age of which we have no historic record, but of which Chinese architecture, with its strange peaks and curves, offers us more than a suggestion,—the great Nomad Era."

There were only two more of Hearn's letters on the exposition, one on March 14, on Mexico at New Orleans, telling of the wax figures, depicting various Mexican types, and describing the feather-work, imitated from that of the Aztecs; the other, appearing April 11, 1885, telling of the government exhibit. On November 7 he wound up his letters *for Harper's* by telling something about "The Last of the Voudoos,"—Jean Montanet, or Voudoo John, or Bayou John, who had just died in New Orleans.

On March 28 and April 4 there appeared in *Harper's Bazar,* some "Notes of a Curiosity Hunter," in which he described some of the things that interested him most in the Japanese and Mexican exhibits.

CPSIA information can be obtained
at www.ICGtesting.com
Printed in the USA
LVHW030139271222
735871LV00001B/274